To:

This book is dedicated to my mother and my family who she has so proudly fed over so many years; to Michelle, not only my rock but the most beautiful woman on earth; Christina, Jean (jnr), Jacques, my father and my brother Anthony, all of whom have helped, contributed and supported me in the creation of this wonderful book and have made me, just simply, the happiest man.

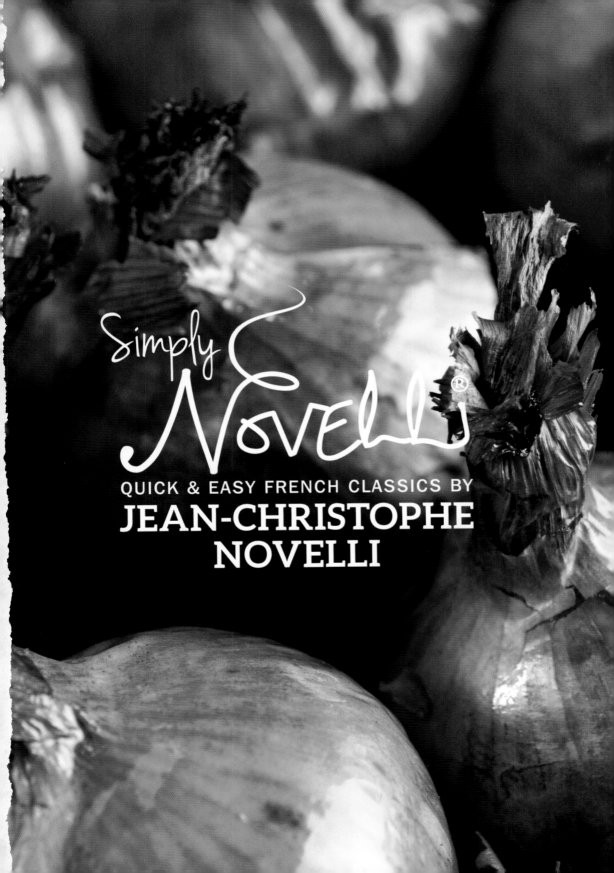

Simply Novelli®

QUICK & EASY FRENCH CLASSICS BY

JEAN-CHRISTOPHE NOVELLI

Pictured left to right: Kit Maharajh, Felice Tocchini, Patti Sloley and Jenny Gibbs

Merci beaucoup...

This book would have been more difficult to create without the help and support from my loyal staff and friends around me.

My residential chefs

Felice Tocchini - he is definitely one of the most consistent and best chefs I have worked with, as well as being a real gentleman.

Patti Sloley - I regard her as my culinary spiritual sister and an oceanic breath of fresh air.

Manju Malhi - one of the most defined, knowledgeable and explicit Indian chefs I have had the pleasure of working with.

Trish Davies - the perfect traditional British cooking expert. Her amazing teaching skills are such an asset to the Academy.

Staff and friends

Jenny Gibbs - supports me throughout all areas of the running of both the Academy and Novelli Associates - sometimes without the true recognition that she rightly deserves.

Iwona Abramczyk, Joanna Lukanus and Jill Taylor - without the background staff at the Academy, the place wouldn't be able to look so good everyday.

Anthony - merci bien to my brother. He made a massive contribution with research for this wonderful book.

Dayan Maharajh - a special thanks goes to Kit's wife, who has helped immensely, not only with the book but she has been an invaluable support for Michelle, the boys and me during this very busy time.

And finally, **Kit Maharajh** - someone I have had the pleasure of knowing for many years and who I truly class as a very dear friend indeed - he is like another brother to me. I have worked with Kit for several years now and he has not only been a big support to the foundations of my organisation, but has also been hugely involved in driving 'Simply Novelli' from inception to the end result. Kit is fondly regarded as the 'heartbeat' of this book.

Bonjour et bienvenue to my latest book!

My quest in these pages is to eliminate the myth that preparing French food can be complicated and daunting. I want to encourage more people, in the country where I have lived for many happy years, to try some of the most famous French classics ever created.

Being a passionate Frenchman, I am very proud of my country's culinary heritage and I wanted to take this opportunity to guide you through our regional cuisine so you can create the wonderful dishes you may have tried and enjoyed on visits to France in your own home.

I have thought about how French classics - created by my gifted predecessors rather than me - have evolved over the centuries. I have brought them into the 21st Century, acknowledging the amazing produce now available from around the world.

I have adapted the recipes for today's busy lifestyles and combined them with my own ambition to create a healthier and quicker method of preparing these classic French dishes, as I have shown so many of my visitors over the last 10 years at The Novelli Academy Cookery School, in the beautiful Hertfordshire village, Tea Green.

It is where I remind my students that food should not only be a necessity in life, but also an experience to express mixed emotions and pleasures - even from something relatively simple.

By following these recipes, people experiencing the joy of cooking for the first time will be able to learn how to impress family and friends with their new found skills. Those of you who are experienced cooks looking for inspiration, be it as a hobby or professionally, can hopefully use my techniques and tips to expand your cooking horizons.

The ultimate aim of Simply Novelli is for all who attempt the recipes to have fun and enjoy cooking the dishes. Once you have succeeded in achieving the results that make you happy, let your imagination and tastebuds direct you through your own versions of these fabulous recipes, remembering only YOU know how your version should look and taste!

Bon appétit et bon chance!

First published in Great Britain in 2013 by Relish Publications.

Copyright © Jean-Christophe Novelli 2013.

The right of Jean-Christophe Novelli to be identified as the
Author of the Work has been asserted by him in accordance
with the Copyright, Designs and Patents Act 1988.

All rights reserved. No part of this publication may be
reproduced, stored in a retrieval system, or transmitted, in any
form or by any means without the prior written permission of
the publisher, nor be otherwise circulated in any form of binding
or cover other than that in which it is published and without a
similar condition being imposed on the subsequent purchaser.

ISBN: 978-0-9575370-3-3

Co-ordinated by Teresa Peters
Design by Vicki Brown
Photography by Tim Green, www.timgreenphotographer.co.uk
Edited by Paul Robertson

Printed in Slovenia on behalf of Latitude Press.

Relish Publications
Shield Green Farm
Tritlington
Morpeth
Northumberland
NE61 3DX

www.relishpublications.co.uk

Contents

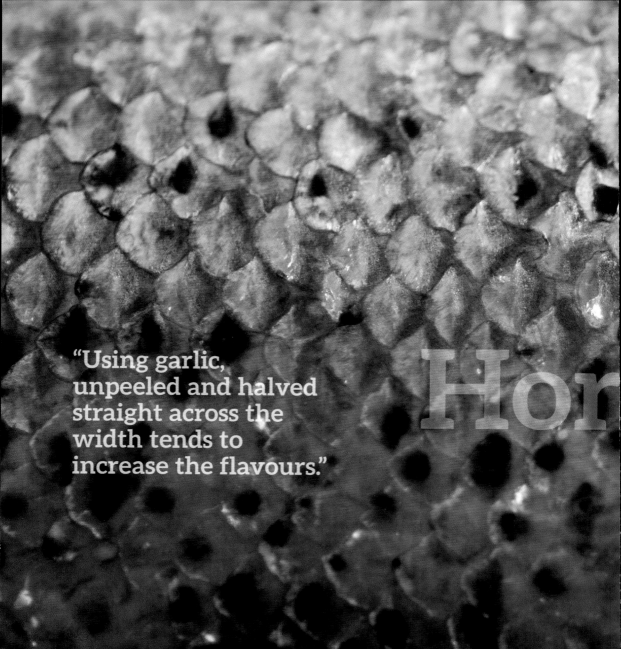

"Using garlic, unpeeled and halved straight across the width tends to increase the flavours."

Hor

d'Oeuvres
To Start

Potage Dubarry
Cauliflower Soup with Reblochon Cheese

This is one of my favourite soups for a cold winter's day and a great one for the kids - very healthy!

Serves: **4**
Preparation Time: **30 minutes**
Cooking Time: **45 minutes**

Ingredients

1 cauliflower (separate the florets)
1 leek (sliced)
50g plain flour
100ml crème fraîche
750ml hot, strong vegetable stock
1 tsp honey
3 tbsp extra virgin rapeseed oil
½ lemon (juice of)
grated nutmeg (pinch of)
150g Reblochon
(cubed and partly frozen)

1 tbsp extra virgin olive oil
1 clove garlic (crushed)
1 tbsp parsley (chopped)
crushed black pepper (to taste)

Chef's Tip

Any hard, strong melting cheese can be used for this recipe. It must be very cold and placed into the bowls at the very last minute before serving for the best taste and effect.

Method

Pick a handful of cauliflower florets and place to one side. These will be used for a garnish when serving.

Roughly chop the remaining cauliflower. Heat the rapeseed oil in a deep, hot pan then sweat the chopped cauliflower with the leeks for 5 minutes. Add the honey and lemon juice. Reduce the heat, making sure the cauliflower and leeks don't colour.

Mix the nutmeg with the flour and add to the vegetables. Stir with a wooden spatula, then add the hot stock. Bring to the boil. Reduce to a simmer for 40 minutes. Remove from the heat.

Using a hand blender, blend everything in the pan and gradually mix in the crème fraîche.

In a separate pan, either steam or boil the reserved florets for no more than 5 minutes, or until the florets look translucent. Strain.

To Serve

Infuse the olive oil with the crushed garlic and herbs.

Ladle the hot soup into your bowls. Dress with a couple of steamed florets in each bowl. Add a few cubes of the very cold cheese and finally, top with a tablespoon of the garlic and herb infused olive oil.

Potée à la Saucisse de Morteau
Smoked Cured Sausage & Vegetable Soup

This dish is normally made in a covered clay pot, over a low heat, and with good quality sausage.

Serves: **4**
Preparation Time: **10 minutes**
Cooking Time: **60 minutes**

Ingredients

500g saucisse de morteau (diced into 8 pieces)
1 carrot (sliced)
1 leek (sliced)
400g Savoy cabbage (sliced)
1 onion (sliced)
½ celeriac (grated - optional, see tip)
1 clove garlic (crushed)
boiling hot water (as required)
4 eggs (poached just before serving)
1 tbsp extra virgin rapeseed oil
½ tsp cumin seeds
4 leaves sage
1 tbsp extra virgin olive oil
150g lentils or white beans (optional - see tip)

Method

Sweat the carrot, leek, cabbage, onion and garlic in a deep, hot pan, with a lid. After 2 minutes, add the sausage and then cover everything with hot water. Add the sage leaves and cumin, bring to the boil and reduce to a simmer for about 30 minutes.

In another pan, poach the 4 eggs just before serving.

To Serve
Serve the soup in a tureen or bowl. Carefully place the poached eggs into the soup and drizzle with a little of the olive oil. Take special care not to ruin the effect by breaking the poached eggs when plating up.

Chef's Tip

Adding half a grated celeriac at the same time as the other vegetables will increase the sweetness of this dish.
150g of lentils or white beans can also be added.

Soupe à la Courgette et Roquefort
Courgette & Roquefort Soup

My take on a marriage of perfectly balanced ingredients.

Serves: **4**
Preparation Time: **15 minutes**
Cooking Time: **30 minutes**

Ingredients

1kg courgette (diced into 2cm cubes)
1 tbsp extra virgin rapeseed oil
4 cloves garlic (crushed)
1 tsp fennel seeds
1 tsp honey
500ml hot, strong vegetable stock
ground black pepper
100ml crème fraîche
1 tbsp chervil stalks
30g Roquefort cheese (cubed and kept in the fridge until required)

Chef's Tip

Add the cubes of cheese at the very last moment before serving. This will ensure the cheese reaches melting point just at the right time.

Method

Heat the rapeseed oil in a deep pan, with a lid. Add the courgettes, garlic and fennel seeds and sweat for 10 minutes, taking care not to let them change colour (if they start to colour, reduce the heat). Add the honey and sauté for approx 2 minutes. Add the stock and a grind of black pepper. Bring to the boil and simmer for 10 minutes. Remove from the heat.

Blend the soup using a hand blender and gradually add the crème fraîche.

To Serve
Run the chervil stalks under very cold water to make sure they are nice and crisp.

Using either 1 large serving bowl or individual bowls, ladle out the hot soup. Add the cheese cubes and place the chervil over the cheese. Serve immediately.

Soupe à l'Ail
Garlic Soup

This is a popular dish in the French Alps, eaten by skiers on the slopes visiting slope-side chalet restaurants for lunch or aprés ski.

Serves: **4**
Preparation Time: **10 minutes**
Cooking Time: **30 minutes**

Ingredients

8 bulbs garlic (peeled and cracked)
2 shallots (sliced)
1 tbsp extra virgin olive oil
2 bay leaves
1 sprig thyme
750ml beef, or strong vegetable stock
1 tsp mustard seeds
1 tsp horseradish sauce
4 anchovy fillets (finely chopped)
½ tsp honey
smoked paprika (pinch of)
2 egg yolks (beaten)
1 tbsp crème fraîche

Chef's Tip

For a really deep flavour, or as an alternative, I like to use smoked garlic in this dish.

Method

Using a hot deep pan, with a lid, add a tablespoon of oil, all the garlic, shallots, bay leaves and thyme and sweat for 2 minutes. Then add the hot stock. Cover and bring to the boil for 10-15 minutes. Remove from the heat and allow to rest with the lid on for approx 15 minutes. After resting, remove the bay leaves, thyme and a few pieces of the garlic.

Whisk in the anchovies, mustard seeds, horseradish, honey and smoked paprika. In a separate bowl, whisk the eggs and introduce this into the soup. Using a hand blender or liquidiser, blend the soup and then return to the heat, adding the reserved pieces of garlic and herbs and stirring continuously. As soon as the soup starts to reach boiling temperature, remove from the heat.

To Serve
Place the very hot soup into a serving tureen and pour a little crème fraîche into the middle. Serve immediately.

Soupe à l'Oignon
Traditional French Onion Soup

Serves: **4**
Preparation Time: **15 minutes**
Cooking Time: **80 minutes**
Best made 24 hours in advance

Ingredients

10 large onions (whole, skin on)
2 tbsp sugar or 1 tbsp honey
2 sprigs thyme
2 bay leaves
2 sprigs rosemary (optional)
2 sage leaves (optional)
crushed black pepper (to taste)
1 bottle (750ml) red wine
150ml strong vegetable stock
(only if required)

4 slices toasted French bread
250g Gruyère cheese
(or other strong, melting hard
cheese - cubed)

Chef's Tip

One of the most important parts of this dish is to create a good stock base. Also, the longer you caramelise the onions the deeper the colour of the finished soup. Ideally, the soup should be made a day in advance, to allow all the flavours to be extracted and infuse - but I know this isn't always possible!

According to history, this soup was based on an original Roman soup recipe, but was changed by Louis XV during a hunting trip where the only provisions he had were onions and Champagne.

Method

Preheat oven to 180°C (fan), 200°C (non-fan), or gas mark 6.

For The Onions
Place the onions on a baking tray with their skins on and whole. Bake in the oven for 10 minutes, then reduce the temperature to 120°C (fan), 140°C (non-fan), or gas mark 1, for 1 hour. Remove from the oven and let the onions cool a little. Over a deep, large pot with tight fitting lid, squeeze the onions with your hands, one by one, carefully extracting the juices and at the same time removing the skins. This will help infuse more flavour into the soup by extracting flavour from the skins. Discard the skins and put the onions in the pot.

For The Soup
Add the sugar, thyme, bay leaves (rosemary and sage if using) and crushed pepper to taste. Sauté to caramelise the onions and then cover all the ingredients with red wine. Bring to the boil and immediately reduce to a simmer. Simmer slowly for 30-40 minutes with the lid on, allowing the condensation to become part of the soup. Don't lift the lid too often (glass lids help if you are intrigued to see what's happening!).

It's best to let the soup cool down first in the fridge, as this allows the true flavours to infuse to give you a true taste. Depending on the type of wine used, you may find that you will need to add more sugar to reduce the acidity of the soup.

To Serve
Reheat the soup to a simmer. Check the taste. If you feel that after heating it's still too strong, add 150ml of stock.

Toast the bread and cut into croutons - the same size as the cheese. Ladle the soup into large bowls and place equal numbers of croutons and cheese straight into the soup so that the cheese starts melting in the soup, just as you serve it.

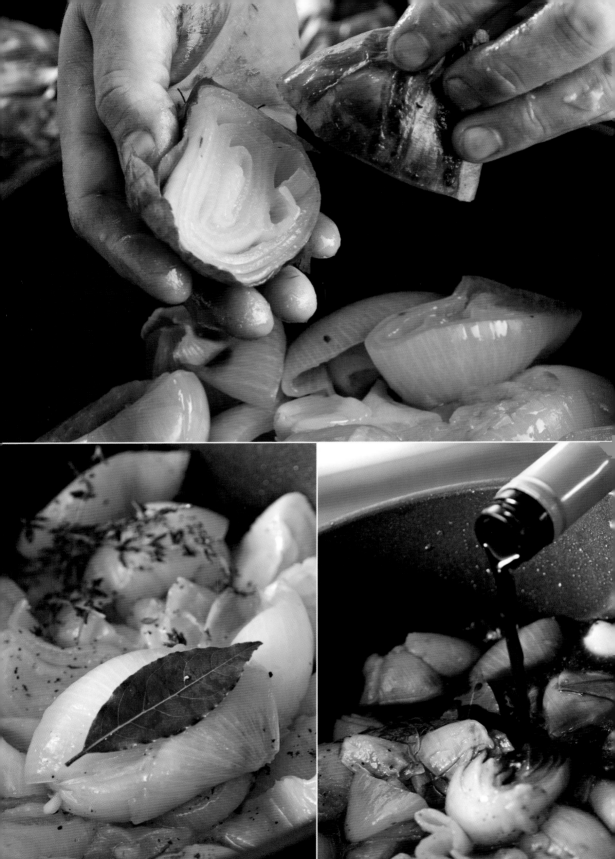

Soupe Verte Spéciale
Special Green Vegetable Soup

This soup is full of folic acid, vitamin E, antioxidants and fibre.
My kids love eating it because of the vivid colour!

Serves: **4**
Preparation Time: **25 minutes**
Cooking Time: **15 minutes**

Ingredients

2 tbsp extra virgin rapeseed oil
3 shallots (sliced)
1 medium sized leek
(halved lengthways)
4 small courgettes
(quartered lengthways)
1 bulb garlic (halved)
smoked paprika (pinch of)
crushed black pepper
1 tsp granulated sugar
4 baby turnips
(halved, with the stalks on)
700ml hot, strong vegetable
stock (or chicken stock)
4 Swiss chard leaves
(washed and sliced)
6 Savoy cabbage leaves
(washed and sliced)
80g fresh peas (podded)
80g fresh broad beans (podded)
150g fresh spinach
2 spring onions (halved lengthways)
60g fresh watercress
2 bay leaves

Infused Oil
3 tbsp extra virgin olive oil
handful of fresh green herbs
(eg basil, oregano, parsley or chervil)

Method

Infuse the olive oil with the green herbs.

Heat the rapeseed oil in a deep pan. Add the shallots, leeks, courgettes, garlic, smoked paprika, black pepper and sugar. Sauté, with a lid on, for 5 minutes without letting it colour. Add the baby turnips, bay leaves and stock. Bring to the boil and simmer for 10 minutes.

In the meantime, clean the chard and cabbage leaves - trim off the stalks and slice across the leaves. Add these to the soup, along with the beans and peas. Simmer for a further 5 minutes, then add the spinach for 1 minute. Add the watercress and spring onions and immediately turn off the heat. Pour the infused oil into the soup and let it stand for a couple of minutes before serving.

Chef's Tip

If you can find courgette flowers, you can stuff these with risotto and cheese and present on top of the soup when serving. (See risotto recipe on page 190).

23

Mouclade des Boucholeurs
Shetland Blue Shell Mussels

Serves: **4**
Preparation Time: **30 minutes**
Plus 3 hours to clean mussels
Cooking Time: **15 minutes**

Ingredients

1½kg Shetland blue shell mussels
(if in season - if not, normal live rope
mussels can be used)
100g oats
1 large Portobello mushroom
(soaked in a bowl of cold water for at
least 30 minutes before using)
2 tbsp extra virgin rapeseed oil
3 shallots (finely sliced)
1 sprig thyme
1 bulb garlic
(halved width-ways with peel on)
½ tbsp honey
1 bay leaf
½ tsp nutmeg (grated)
½ tsp ground turmeric
1 tsp mild curry powder
250ml crème fraîche
1 sprig tarragon
1 tsp plain flour
250ml Muscadet or dry
white wine
crushed black pepper (to taste)
fresh green herbs (chopped)
crusty bread

Method

For The Mussels
Place the mussels and oats in a large bowl. Cover them completely with cold water and leave for at least 3 hours. This will clean the mussels and reduce any grittiness. After 3 hours, remove the mussels and strain through a colander by lifting the shells out by hand and placing them into the colander to prevent sand entering the sauce. Rinse under cold water.

For The Mushroom
Remove the mushroom from the water, squeeze lightly and dice.

To Cook The Mussels
Place a large pan, big enough to hold 3 times the number of mussels, with a tight fitting lid, on a high heat. Add the rapeseed oil, sliced shallots, thyme, garlic halves, honey, bay leaf, nutmeg, turmeric, diced mushrooms and curry powder. Stir for about 5 minutes. Then add the mussels, cover with the lid and cook for another 5 minutes, or until the mussels just start to open. Once they start opening, only cook for a further 30 seconds.

Using a colander placed over a bowl, strain the mussels and all the ingredients. Cover the colander with clingfilm.

Chef's Tip

If you are in a hurry, mix a little cooking liquor with some flour to make a paste. Add that back into the sauce to help speed up the thickening process.
If the mussel shells used are small, don't waste time splitting the shells, just serve!

This is an Atlantic coast speciality due to the many mussel farms there.

To Prepare The Sauce

Replace the strained liquid into the original pan and bring to the boil on a high heat. Reduce the liquid until it has a thick consistency. Add the wine, crème fraîche and tarragon. Taste the sauce and adjust the seasoning to suit your taste. Remove from the heat and cover.

In the meantime, pick out half of the mussels that look good, (large and juicy), and place to one side to help with your presentation. Remove the rest of the mussels from their shells and place into the warm sauce.

To Serve

Take off half of the shell of each of the reserved mussels and place around your serving bowl. Then, ladle the remaining mussels and sauce into the bowl. Decorate with some chopped green herbs and serve immediately with fresh, warm crusty bread.

Coquilles St Jacques
Poached Scallops with a Mushroom Sauce

Serves: **4**
Preparation Time: **20 minutes**
Cooking Time: **10 minutes**

Ingredients

4 fresh scallops in their shells
(cleaned and ready to remove - a good
fishmonger should be obliging!)
**1.2kg freshly washed baby
spinach** (patted dry in kitchen paper or
a dry cloth)
mild curry powder (pinch of)
10 chestnut mushrooms
(wiped with a dry cloth and finely sliced -
do not wash)
grated nutmeg (pinch of)
4 cloves fresh garlic (crushed)
1 tsp honey
1 tsp cornflour
50g mature Cheddar cheese
(or any other hard strong cheese,
grated - optional)
80ml dry white wine (optional)
crushed black pepper (to taste)

Method

You will need a non-stick pan, with a tight fitting lid, and a wooden spatula.

To Cook The Spinach
Heat the pan on a high heat with nothing in it. When it's hot, add the grated nutmeg and curry powder, followed by the 4 crushed garlic cloves and the spinach. Add the teaspoon of honey and a grind of black pepper. Cover with the lid and leave to wilt.

Providing the spinach was a little moist before using, there should be a fair amount of liquid produced from the spinach - the condensation on the lid of the pan will form part of the sauce - so do not lift the lid too often.

After approx 1 minute, stir quickly with a wooden spatula. Remove the pan from the heat. Using a fine sieve placed over a bowl, drain the spinach being careful to retain all the liquor in the bowl. Cover the sieve with clingfilm to retain the heat, while still draining.

Chef's Tip

This recipe can be prepared a day or so in advance and placed in a fridge. Remove the scallops 30 minutes before they are due to be finished and bake for 10 minutes just before serving. One scallop per person should be enough as a starter as the sauce is quite rich.

Coquilles St Jacques is the French word for 'scallops' and is often described in classic terms as poached scallops in white wine. This dish was incredibly popular in French restaurants in New York during the 1950s. In my own method of preparing this classic, I have tried to reduce the fat content throughout the dish, just using the fat from the cheese, and I have eliminated the salt too.

For The Scallops

Put the same pan on a high heat and add some of the spinach liquid from the bowl. Add the scallops and cook on each side for 30 seconds. Carefully remove the scallops and add them to the spinach. Re-cover with clingfilm.

For The Mushrooms

Place the pan back on a high heat and add the sliced mushrooms. Add some of the spinach liquid and cook for 1 minute, stirring occasionally. Remove the mushrooms, using a slotted spoon to a plate, and cover with clingfilm.

For The Sauce

Mix a teaspoon of cornflour with a little of the spinach liquid (approx 1 tbsp) in a bowl to create a thick paste. Add the paste to the liquid left over from cooking the mushrooms and add any further liquid that has been strained from the spinach. Bring to the boil over a high heat. Stir with a wooden spoon and reduce to approx 125ml. Once the sauce is thick enough to coat the back of the spoon, remove from the heat and, when warm, add the cheese and wine (optional) and stir.

To Serve

Preheat the oven to 180ºC (fan), 200ºC (non-fan), gas mark 6.

Lay out the scallop shells on an oven tray. Place a little cooked spinach on the shell (no liquid), a little of the mushroom on top of the spinach, followed by the cooked scallop. Then, using a large spoon, cover with the cheese sauce. Pour in one movement so that the sauce drips down covering the entire scallop.

Heat in the oven for 10 minutes. Serve immediately.

Crevettes Grises & Artichauts
Baked Smoked Shrimps with Artichokes

This type of dish is commonly eaten in the Eastern Pyrenees of southern France.

Serves: **4**
Preparation Time: **35 minutes**
Cooking Time: **30 minutes**

Ingredients

4 large artichokes (stalks removed)
200g smoked shrimps
(crevettes grises)
½ lemon (juice of)
1 tsp sugar
2 shallots (sliced)
6 cloves garlic (crushed)
½ tsp smoked paprika
1 egg
150g Gruyère or Beaufort
cheese (grated)
1 tbsp extra virgin rapeseed oil
6 plum tomatoes (chopped)
1 tsp honey
½ tsp cumin seeds
1 sprig thyme
80g caper berries (in brine)
150g crème fraîche
3 tbsp extra virgin olive oil
1 tbsp chervil and basil leaves
(chopped)
1 bunch watercress

Method

Preheat the oven to 160ºC (fan), 180ºC (non-fan), or gas mark 4.

To Cook The Artichokes
Add the artichokes, sugar and lemon juice to a large, deep pan filled with enough water to cover. Bring to the boil. Allow to simmer for 15 minutes, strain and allow to cool. When cooled, remove the outside leaves of the artichoke, then the furry part of the vegetable, leaving just the artichoke hearts. Keep to one side.

For The Shrimps
In a sauté pan, heat a little rapeseed oil and sweat the shallots, half the garlic and the smoked paprika for approx 3 minutes. Add the shrimps and sauté for 1 minute. Strain everything from the pan through a fine sieve and into a bowl to retain the liquid. In another bowl, beat the egg, add the cheese and introduce the crème fraîche. Mix with the shrimp mixture and stir.

For The Tomato Mixture
In another pan, heat a little oil and add the tomatoes, cumin, thyme, honey and the rest of the garlic. Sauté for about 5 minutes. Add the caper berries, including some of the juice, and reduce the liquid slowly over a medium heat. Add the olive oil and herbs, except the watercress. Spoon into a gratin dish.

To Finish The Dish Just Before Serving
Layer the artichoke hearts on top of the tomato mixture. Spoon the cheese and shrimp mixture over the artichoke hearts to approx twice the height of the artichoke. Transfer to the oven for 30 minutes.

To Serve
Garnish with a little bunch of watercress placed over each artichoke. Everything should be kept upright and tall.

33

Escabèche de Maquereaux
Cold Cured Mackerel

The mackerel in this dish requires no cooking but needs to be prepared the day before serving to get the best results.

Serves: **4**
Preparation Time: **15 minutes**
Cooking Time: **15 minutes**
Best made 24 hours in advance

Ingredients

4 mackerel
(whole, cleaned and heads removed)
2 carrots
(thinly sliced lengthways into batons)
1 onion (thinly sliced)
1 stalk celery (thinly sliced lengthways)
10-12 radishes (sliced)
1 star anise
1 tbsp fennel seeds
1 tsp coriander seeds
10 cloves
1 sprig thyme
20 black peppercorns
4 cloves garlic (crushed)
1 unwaxed lemon (juice of)
400ml dry white wine
100ml cider vinegar
6 cornichon gherkins (diced)
2 tsp capers (chopped)
1 tsp fresh dill (chopped)

Method

Arrange the mackerel, in a line, in a dish suitable for the fridge.

Sauté the onions without using any fat in a deep, heated pan with the lid on. Gradually add all the other ingredients, stirring continuously. Bring to the boil, then simmer for 5 minutes. Pour over the fish, covering immediately with clingfilm. Place into the fridge for up to 24 hours if possible.

Serve chilled with slices of toasted bread.

Chef's Tip

If you do not like mackerel, any fish fillets can be used.

Gratin de Coquilles St Jacques avec Fromage Bleu
Minute Scallops with Endive & Blue Cheese

A speciality from Aveyron which was reputed to be served to the pilgrims en route to St Jacques de Compostela.

Serves: **4**
Preparation Time: **15 minutes**
Cooking Time: **15 minutes**

Ingredients

4 large scallops
(in their shells - ask your fishmonger to prepare the scallops for cooking)
1 tbsp extra virgin rapeseed oil
1 large baking apple
(unpeeled, cored and finely sliced)
1 endive or chicory (finely sliced)
1 small leek (finely sliced)
1 tbsp Cognac
100ml Noilly Prat or dry white wine
150ml crème fraîche
1 tbsp parsley or chervil (chopped)
40g Roquefort or Stilton cheese
(cubed)

Method

For The Scallops
Open and clean the scallops (if your fishmonger hasn't already helped you with this!). Separate the flesh from the shell and keep to one side.

Fry the scallops for 1 minute on each side in the rapeseed oil in a hot pan. Remove and reserve for later.

To Make The Blue Cheese Sauce
Using the same pan and no extra oil, introduce the sliced endive, leek and apple. Sweat for 2 minutes on a high heat and covered with a lid. Carefully add the Cognac and ignite with a flame to flambé.

Add the wine (or Noilly Prat) and reduce the heat to a simmer. Reduce the sauce by about one third, then add the crème fraîche, cheese and chopped green herbs.

Return the scallops to the pan and immediately turn off the heat.

To Serve
Carefully remove each scallop, cover with the sauce to glaze and finish with the parsley or chervil.

Chef's Tip

You can prepare the scallops in advance, cover with clingfilm and keep in the fridge until ready to cook. The sauce can also be made in advance and warmed through before adding the scallops at the final stage.

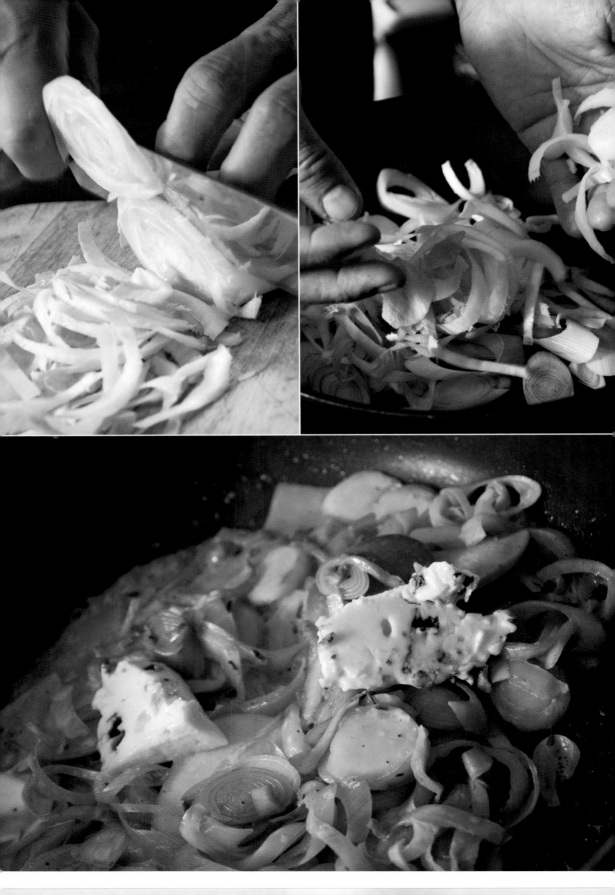

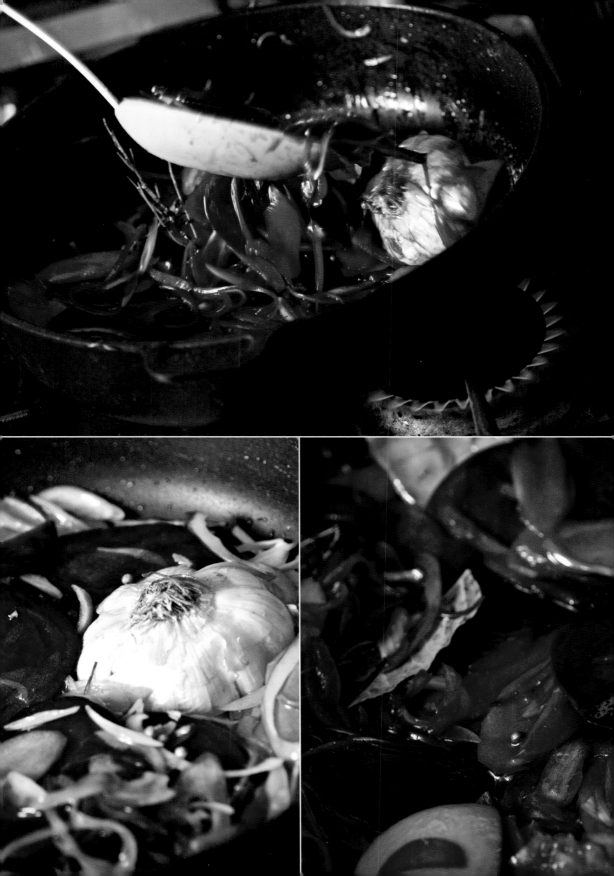

Moules Marinières
Mussels in White Wine & Cream Sauce

Serves: **4**
Preparation Time: **10 minutes**
Plus 3 hours to clean mussels
Cooking Time: **10 minutes**

Ingredients

1½kg fresh mussels (in their shells)
100g oats
¹/₃ tsp mild curry powder
2 onions (finely diced)
2 bay leaves
1 sprig fresh thyme
2 tsp honey
1 bulb garlic (cut in half)
4 tbsp dry white wine or
Vermouth (optional)
125ml low fat crème fraîche or
double cream
fresh herbs (basil, tarragon, parsley,
or any other green herbs)
1 tbsp cold pressed extra virgin
olive oil (to sweat the onions)
crushed black pepper (to taste)
1 tbsp cold pressed extra virgin
olive oil (optional)

Method

For The Mussels
Using the same cleaning method as the Mouclade des Boucholeurs (page 24), place all the mussels and oats into a large bowl and cover them completely with cold water for at least 3 hours. This will clean the mussels and reduce the chance of having gritty mussels. After 3 hours, remove the mussels and strain through a colander by lifting the shells out by hand and placing them into the colander to prevent sand entering the sauce. Rinse under cold water.

Chef's Tip

In some parts of France, especially the north, mussels are served as a main course with pommes frites or sliced baguettes.

Always make sure that you use a pan approx 3 times the size of the mussels being cooked to allow for the shells opening.

According to legend, an Irishman called Patrick Walton showed French men how to grow mussels on submerged wood piles after wrecking his ship on the French coast.

Heat the onions, curry powder, bay leaves, thyme and a grind of black pepper in a deep, very hot pan, with a tight fitting lid, with olive oil. Cover and sweat for about 3 minutes, keeping the cover on at all times to generate some moisture. Add the mussels, replace the lid and shake the pan. Add the honey and garlic, replace the lid and shake again. Once you notice the shells opening, remove from the heat. Pour the contents of the pan through a sieve placed over a large bowl. Clingfilm the strained mussels to retain the heat.

For The Sauce
Pour the liquid drained from the mussels into the original pan and place on a medium heat. Reduce by approx one third. Add the same amount of wine or Vermouth (if using) and reduce the sauce again. Once you have a thick consistency, which covers the back of a spoon, remove from the heat.

Add the same amount of crème fraîche or double cream as the amount of sauce, then add the mussels. Mix thoroughly. Add all of the herbs and any other liquid that may have been strained from the mussels.

If you want the sauce to have a little extra richness, add 1 tablespoon of good quality, extra virgin olive oil just before serving.

Quenelles de Poisson
Poached Mixed fish

Originating in Lyon in the 1900s, these quenelles were originally made with bone marrow but I think, and hope you agree, that they work really well with fish.

Serves: **4**
Preparation Time: **30 minutes**
Cooking Time: **35 minutes**

Ingredients

200g mixed white fish
(preferably pike, but cod, haddock or even crayfish may be used)
100ml white wine
300ml strong fish stock
(or vegetable or chicken stock)
1 tsp honey
80g cream cheese
(low fat can be used)
cayenne pepper (pinch of)
mild curry powder (pinch of)
60g cornflour
3 eggs
300ml double cream
2 cloves garlic (crushed)
100g strong, hard cheese (such as Gruyère, Beaufort or Cheddar - grated)
100g olives
(Lucques, Picholine, Verdale, Bouteillan, Negrette, Rougette and Aglandeau)

Chef's Tip

I often serve the quenelles by wrapping them in a lightly steamed Savoy cabbage leaf after poaching in the stock and before baking. They can also be served with the tomato sauce left over from making my tomato and vanilla infused oil (see page 106).

Method

For The Special Béchamel Sauce
Heat the white wine in a hot, deep pan for 5 minutes to remove the acidity. Add 150ml of the stock, the honey and the cream cheese. Stir thoroughly with a wooden spatula, but take care not to let it boil. Add the cayenne pepper and curry powder and continue to stir. Add the cornflour and mix vigorously, over a low heat, to avoid the mixture sticking to the base of the pan - this will also help evaporate the water from the mixture. Once a dough has started to form, add 2 eggs, one by one, and mix in with the wooden spoon. Leave to one side to cool, uncovered. When cool, add 40ml of the cream and 1 clove of crushed garlic. Mix thoroughly. This is the béchamel sauce which will be used to cover the quenelles when serving.

To Prepare The Fish
Put all the fish into a blender and blend for 10 seconds. Add 1 egg and blend for a further 10 seconds. Stir in the remaining cream and another clove of crushed garlic. Place in the fridge to chill until ready to use.

To Serve
Preheat the oven to 160ºC (fan), 180ºC (non-fan), or gas mark 4.

Heat the remaining 150ml of fish stock in a deep pan.

Using two large serving spoons, turn some of the fish mixture into quenelles. This is easier to manage if you run your spoons under very hot water before shaping the quenelle. Place them, one by one, into the stock and cook for 5 minutes. Carefully remove with a slotted spoon and place into a baking dish.

Cover the quenelles with the béchamel sauce, the grated cheese and the olives. Cook in the oven for 15 minutes. Garnish with herbs of your choice and serve.

53

Salade Niçoise
Tuna Salad Niçoise

Hailing from Nice in the South of France, this salad combines everything that originated from and around the Mediterranean.

Serves: **4**
Preparation Time: **15 minutes**
Cooking Time: **20 minutes**

Ingredients

50g artichoke hearts (you can use tinned, but fresh, blanched is better)
50g palm hearts (finely sliced)
8 baby new potatoes (halved)
4 x 150g tuna steaks
1 tbsp extra virgin olive oil
150g French beans
4 eggs
3 plum tomatoes (quartered)
6 anchovy fillets
2-3 gem lettuces (separated and placed in ice cold water until needed)
12 black olives
2 tbsp fresh parsley and basil (chopped)
1 red onion (halved and finely sliced)
8 whole caper berries
1 sprig rosemary
cracked black pepper
seasoning (to taste)
3 tbsp vinaigrette dressing (see page 114)

Method

For The Potatoes, Eggs And Green Beans
Place the unpeeled potatoes in a pan of boiling water with the sprig of rosemary for 10 minutes. Add the eggs and boil for a further 4 minutes. Finally, add the French beans and continue boiling for 3 more minutes.

Strain everything and refresh the eggs under cold water. Peel the eggs, slice in half lengthways and keep to one side. Cover the beans and potatoes with clingfilm.

For The Tuna
Heat a pan with 1 tbsp olive oil and sear each side of the tuna steak for 1 minute. Place on kitchen paper until needed.

To Serve
Place the lettuce leaves, beans, potatoes, tomatoes, olives, red onion, caper berries, all the chopped herbs, anchovy fillets, palm hearts, artichoke hearts and eggs in a salad bowl and add a grind of black pepper to taste. Spoon over the vinaigrette (see page 114) dressing. Wash your hands and carefully mix the salad, using your hands by lifting the salad from the bottom and turning it over. Serve with the tuna steak on top of the salad.

Chef's Tip

Although Niçoise is traditionally made with tuna, roast or blanched chicken may be used instead. Chilling the lettuce leaves overnight in ice cold water in your fridge will make them even crisper.

Soufflé au Poisson
Fish Soufflé

This typically French dish has evolved over the centuries and there are many existing variations.

Serves: **4**
Preparation Time: **15 minutes**
Cooking Time: **40 minutes**

Ingredients

200g any firm, white fish
50ml extra virgin rapeseed oil
60g plain flour
100ml fish or vegetable stock
saffron (pinch of)
1 clove garlic (crushed)
few sprigs fresh coriander
6 egg whites
2 anchovy fillets
(chopped, optional, see tip)
1 tsp horseradish sauce
(optional, see tip)
1 tsp mustard (optional, see tip)

4 small ramekin dishes,
or 1 large dish (chilled)

Chef's Tip

For additional flavour, add either the chopped anchovies, mustard or horseradish to the béchamel sauce before spooning into the ramekins. You may also leave half the fish out of the béchamel and introduce this after the béchamel has been put into the ramekins for a different effect.

Method

For The Fish

Preheat oven to 160ºC (fan), 180ºC (non-fan), or gas mark 4.

Heat the stock in a pan with a lid on and bring to the boil. Add the garlic, coriander sprigs and fish, cover immediately. Set aside and let the mixture infuse for at least 10 minutes.

To Prepare The Soufflé

In a separate pan, add the oil and warm slowly. Add the flour and stir continuously. Add about 40ml of stock from the fish pan and the pinch of saffron and mix thoroughly. Remove from the heat.

Remove the fish from the stock and pat dry with a paper cloth on both sides. Remove the skin and flake into the béchamel sauce. Stir in carefully.

In a mixing bowl, add the egg whites with a minute pinch of salt. Whisk to soft peaks so that they do not run out of the bowl when lifted over your head!

Fold a little of the egg white mixture into the béchamel sauce, a spoonful at a time, until all of the egg whites have been mixed in.

To Cook The Soufflé

Lightly oil 1 large or 4 small ramekin dishes, dust with a little flour and place into the fridge so that they are nice and cold (this can be done in advance). Spoon the mixture equally across the ramekins, making sure that you tap the dish on the worktop every now and then to reduce the chance of air pockets forming.

Place on a baking tray and bake in the oven for 40 minutes, without opening the oven door.

Serve immediately.

Carpaccio Boeuf ou Thon
Beef or Tuna Carpaccio

Carpaccio is the name given to very finely sliced raw meat, fish, vegetables or fruit normally seasoned with lemon juice or a vinaigrette dressing.

Serves: **4**
Preparation Time: **10 minutes**
Curing Time In Fridge/Freezer:
4 hours

Ingredients

500g beef or tuna fillet
(in 1 piece)
3 tbsp wholegrain mustard
(moutarde à l'ancienne)
1 tbsp fresh coriander leaves
(chopped)
1 tbsp fresh mint leaves (chopped)
2 unwaxed lemons (juice of)
3 tbsp extra virgin olive oil
3 tbsp extra virgin rapeseed oil
50g Parmesan cheese (shaved)
100g fresh beansprouts
2cm fresh ginger root
(sliced and unpeeled)
½ tsp coriander seeds
(lightly crushed)
crushed black pepper
150g French beans (boiled)

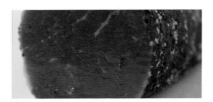

Method

Heat the rapeseed oil in a large sauté pan on a low heat. Add the ginger, coriander seeds, then the beef or tuna. Turning occasionally, fry the beef for 8 minutes, or the tuna for 5 minutes, sealing all sides. Remove from the pan and place to one side.

Wash and chop the coriander, leaving enough moisture so that the leaves stick to your fingers as you cut them. Place on a plate.

When the fillet is still warm (not hot), cover completely with the mustard and roll in the coriander leaves.

Place the meat in the centre of a large sheet of foil and encase the foil around the meat. Twist the ends to form a tight parcel. Place this into the fridge for 2 hours and then the freezer for 2 hours.

To Serve

In a bowl, mix the extra virgin olive oil with the lemon juice and black pepper.

Remove the fillet (beef or tuna) from the freezer and remove the foil. Slice, very thinly, with a sharp knife. Place on a large serving plate and spoon the dressing over the carpaccio. Place a handful of crisp beansprouts and some French beans on top. Finish with Parmesan cheese shavings, the chopped mint and any chopped coriander that you may still have left over.

Chef's Tip

Using foil to wrap the fillet will help to reduce the temperature more quickly than clingfilm. Leave the beansprouts in cold water for half a day then drain 15 minutes before you need them to ensure crispness.

Picarde d'Endives
Chicory Wrapped in Pancetta with a Cheese Sauce

This is a typically northern French dish.

Serves: **4**
Preparation Time: **15 minutes**
Cooking Time: **50 minutes**

Ingredients

8 endives or chicory (large)
8 slices Parma or Serrano ham
3 garlic cloves (crushed)
1 lemon (peeled and juiced)
200g Maroilles, Reblochon,
or Camembert cheese (cubed)
40g unsalted butter, or 50ml
rapeseed oil
50g flour
1 tsp honey
½ tsp grated nutmeg
300g spinach
300ml full-fat milk
100ml dry white wine
ground black pepper (to taste)

Chef's Tip

For a vegetarian option,
the endives can be rolled in a
savoury pancake instead of
smoked ham and the cheese
changed to suit.

Method

For The Chicory

Remove the dry outer leaves from the endives (chicory)
and slice in half lengthways. Place in a large sauté pan,
with a lid.

Place the pan on a low heat and add the butter (or
rapeseed oil if preferred). Grate in some nutmeg,
then add the lemon juice, the lemon peel and the honey.
Gently sauté on a low heat, without letting it change
colour. Bring to the boil and add the white wine. Cover for
35 minutes.

After 35 minutes, carefully remove the endives and
set aside.

For The Spinach

Add the crushed garlic and spinach to the same pan.
Increase the heat to high and cover for 1 minute.
Remove the spinach with a slotted spoon and set aside.

For The Sauce

Add the flour to the pan and mix in thoroughly with a
wooden spatula. Add the milk and stir until this thickens.
Remove from the heat, add some pepper to taste, then
add the cheese.

To Serve

On a flat surface, lay out a sheet of smoked ham and
spread a spoonful of spinach over the ham. Place 2
halves of the endive in the middle and carefully roll the
parcel. Arrange the parcels on a serving dish. Finish the
dish off by pouring the cheese sauce over the endive
parcels. Brown under the grill and serve.

Oignons Farçis aux Champignons
Stuffed Onion with Mushrooms

Two foods that are associated with the French, onions and mushrooms - a perfect combination.

Serves: **4**
Preparation Time: **20 minutes**
Cooking Time: **30 minutes**

Ingredients

4 large onions (St André if available)
2 tbsp extra virgin rapeseed oil
150g mushrooms (shitake, or better still, oyster mushrooms - chopped)
1 sprig thyme
1 sprig sage
3 cloves garlic (crushed)
1 tsp cep powder (see tip)
100g crème fraîche
50g Beaufort cheese (sliced thickly)

Chef's Tip

Sausage meat can be added to the stuffing of the onions. Cep powder can be substituted with any ground, dried mushrooms that may be easier to buy in your local supermarket.

Method

Preheat the oven to 180ºC (fan), 200ºC (non-fan), or gas mark 6.

Steam the onions for 15-20 minutes (depending on the size). Remove from the steamer and carefully slice the top off each onion. Keep to one side for presenting the dish later. When cool to the touch, scoop out some of the flesh from the end that has been sliced off and place in a bowl. Make sure the outer layers of the onion stay intact, for filling later on.

Heat the rapeseed oil in a hot sauté pan. Add the mushrooms, thyme, sage and garlic and sweat for a couple of minutes. Then add the onion pulp and sweat for a further 5 minutes. Slowly dry out the mixture, then add the cep powder and mix thoroughly - creating what's called a 'Duxelles' (paste). When this mixture is completely dry, you will enjoy the fabulous aromas.
At this point, add the crème fraîche and bring to the boil to reduce a little. Set aside to cool.

To Serve
When the onion and Duxelles mixture is cold, spoon back into the onions and place on a baking tray. Bake for 10 minutes. Add the cheese and bake for a further 10 minutes. Serve immediately.

Aubergines Sautées aux Canneberges
Sautéed Aubergine with Cranberries

Serves: **4**
Preparation Time: **20 minutes**
Cooking Time: **35 minutes**

Ingredients

3 aubergines
1 tbsp extra virgin rapeseed oil
1 sprig rosemary
½ bulb garlic
6 cardamom pods
crushed black pepper (to taste)
50ml water
2 Golden Delicious apples
(cored, peeled and diced into large pieces)
½ tsp cumin seeds
2 tbsp honey
150g cranberries (fresh if possible,
otherwise dried or frozen will do)
1 lemon (juice of)
1 tsp peanut oil (optional)
1 sprig fresh mint (snatched)

Method

For The Aubergines
Wash the aubergines before cutting. Trim off the stalk then cut the aubergines lengthways into quarters. Now dice the aubergines into approx 4 pieces across the lengths of aubergine.

Add all the aubergine pieces into a dry, large, hot sauté pan and cover with a lid for 5 minutes. Strain all the liquid from the pan. Then, using a tea towel, pat the aubergines to remove any excess liquid. Return the pan with the aubergines to the heat. Add the rosemary, garlic and cardamom pods then give the pan a shake. Add the rapeseed oil, some black pepper and stir.

Pour a little water into the hot pan, but no more than 50ml at this point. Cover and cook for between 5-8 minutes until the aubergines are cooked, but not soggy. (If the water doesn't start to boil immediately when hitting the pan, add a little less water). The point of this procedure is to avoid creating too much juice or moisture which may remove some of the fantastic flavours that are created at this stage. Pour everything from the pan into a bowl and cover with clingfilm.

To Cook The Apples
Use the same pan on a high heat. Add the apples, cumin and honey then stir thoroughly. Add the cranberries as the colour of the apples starts to change. Reduce the heat before covering with the lid - this will help to steam the fruit. Simmer for approx 15 minutes until the fruit is soft enough to crush. Remove the pan from the heat and lightly crush the apple and cranberries. Drizzle in the peanut oil, (if using), or you can add a teaspoon of rapeseed oil. Taste the apple mixture - if you find it too sweet, add a little squeeze of lemon juice.

Chef's Tip

Keeping any fresh herbs in ice cold water for at least 30 minutes helps to improve the flavours and keeps the herbs fresh. There is a 'tip-clip' on our e-book.

This was an inspiring creation of mine using some unusual combinations of herbs, spices and ingredients, all of which blend perfectly together.

To Serve
Snatch (tear roughly) the mint leaves to release the oils and throw these into the apple mixture. Stir briefly then re-introduce the aubergines into the pan. Heat gently for a short while, turn out into a nice serving dish and serve.

Les Artichauts à la Façon Maman Novelli
Artichokes, Maman Novelli Style

This is a dish that my mother would prepare when we had a house full of visitors, great fun to eat from a rustic dish.

Serves: **4**
Preparation Time: **5 minutes**
Cooking Time: **70 minutes**

Ingredients

Cooking The Artichokes
4 large artichokes
(stalks left on)
1ltr water
sugar (pinch of)
1 lemon (sliced)
2 bay leaves
1 sprig thyme
1 sprig rosemary

Sauce
1 tbsp extra virgin rapeseed oil
10g plain flour
100ml hot cooking liquor
(from the artichoke)
½ lemon (juice of)
1 clove garlic (crushed)
2 tbsp extra virgin olive oil

Chef's Tip

This is also good served with my basic vinaigrette (see page 114). Adding a teaspoon of mustard will change the sauce slightly to give you another type of dip to serve.

Method

For The Artichokes
Boil the water in a deep pan with a lid, then add all the ingredients for cooking the artichokes. Bring to the boil and simmer for approx 30-40 minutes, then leave to cool in the water for 20 minutes. Drain for 10 minutes in a colander. Reserve 100ml of the cooking liquor.

For The Sauce
In a pan, add the rapeseed oil and flour and whisk thoroughly. Then, slowly add the hot cooking liquor and continue whisking until the sauce thickens. Add a squeeze of lemon juice, the crushed garlic and a drizzle of extra virgin olive oil.

To Serve
Place all the artichokes into a large bowl and let your guests peel off the leaves and dip into the sauce, pulling the flesh off the leaves with their teeth. You're then left with the hearts which are exceptionally tasty.

Beignets au Fromage
Feta & Sweet Potato Fritters With a Tomato & Chilli Chutney

Reportedly created by Crusaders in the 13th Century.

Serves: **4**
Preparation Time: **30 minutes**
Cooking Time: **10 minutes**

Ingredients

600g sweet potatoes
(whole, skins on)
4 cloves garlic (crushed)
3 tbsp chilli oil
4 egg yolks (beaten)
8 fresh basil leaves
(chopped - or any green herbs that
you enjoy)
300g Feta cheese
chickpea flour
(also known as gram flour)
rapeseed or vegetable oil for
deepfrying (enough to cover)

Chef's Tip

These fritters and the tomato chilli chutney can be prepared in advance, but are best served just after frying. For a twist on this dish the Feta cheese can be replaced with 300g crabmeat.

Method

Preheat an oven to 180ºC (fan), 200ºC (non-fan), or gas mark 6.

For The Sweet Potatoes
Boil the sweet potatoes in their skins for 20 minutes. Remove and drain, patting dry. Place on a baking tray in the oven for 10 minutes to completely dry them out. This is very important as it achieves the best consistency for later in the recipe.

In a warm pan, add the chilli oil and gently heat for a couple of seconds. Remove from the heat and add the garlic. Take the sweet potatoes and squeeze the flesh out of the skins into the pan and stir. Add the beaten egg yolks and mix thoroughly. Once mixed, add the feta cheese or crabmeat (optional - see tip), stir again, then add the basil and green herbs and mix thoroughly.

For The Fritters
Heat a pan of oil to approx 160ºC.

Wet your hands a little in cold water and, with damp hands, roll a little of the mixture in your hand. Roll in the chickpea flour and fry for 3 minutes. Fry a few at a time and, once all of the mixture has been fried, increase the heat of the oil to approx 200ºC and fry all the fritters again for a further 30 seconds. Drain on kitchen paper before serving.

To Serve
Serve with my tomato chilli chutney (see page 110).

Salade du Midi
French Bean & Goat's Cheese Salad

A tastier way of preparing French beans.

Serves: **4**
Preparation Time: **2 hours**
(including resting in the fridge)
Cooking Time: **6 minutes**

Ingredients

600g haricot verts, French or
green beans
(stalks left on and washed)
3 cloves garlic (crushed)
3½ tbsp extra virgin olive oil
½ tsp fennel seeds
1 tbsp chervil leaves
150g goat's cheese
(cubed and removed from the fridge for
at least 30 minutes before using)
1 tsp honey
1 tbsp extra virgin rapeseed oil
(for frying)
2 slices thick sliced brown bread
(toasted then cubed)
2 tsp sherry vinegar

Method

Place a serving dish into the freezer for at least 1 hour
before using.

To Cook The Green Beans
Heat a non-stick sauté pan, then heat the rapeseed oil.
When very hot, add the fennel seeds, garlic and the
washed beans, then cover with a lid. Shake the pan,
holding the lid on - the hot oil will help remove the excess
water left in the beans. Continue cooking for approx 4
minutes. Remove from the heat. Add the honey and the
goat's cheese and shake again, with the lid on.

Using a slotted spoon, transfer the French bean mix into
the freezing cold serving dish.

To Prepare The Dressing
There should be about a tablespoon of juice left in the
pan. Stir in the same amount of extra virgin olive oil, add
the vinegar, then pour over the beans.

Return to the fridge for between 30-60 minutes.

To Make The Croutons
Using the same pan, fry the cubes of bread in the leftover
oil and juices, on a high heat, until they are crispy.

To Serve
Sprinkle the bread over the beans, along with the chervil
leaves. Serve.

Chef's Tip

If a good quality pan is used, it is nearly impossible
to burn this dish as the beans nearly always steam
in their own juices.

Vichyssoise de Betteraves
Beetroot in a Spicy Orange Reduction

Originally created by a New York based French chef.

Serves: **4**
Preparation Time: **15 minutes**
Cooking Time: **25 minutes**

Ingredients

800g beetroot (peeled and sliced)
500ml orange juice (depending on size of pan, more may be required)
6 cardamom pods
1 tbsp honey
½ tsp mild curry powder
1 tbsp parsley
crushed black pepper (to taste)
1 garlic clove (crushed)
1 tbsp extra virgin olive oil

Chef's Tip

For a fresher flavour in your sauce, use freshly squeezed orange juice, but otherwise carton juice will do. If you have difficulty reducing the orange juice, add a teaspoon of cornflour to help the process along.

To increase the flavour of the cardamom pods, heat a dry pan and place the pods in the pan for a short while and watch the pods swell. The aroma will fill the room.

Method

Place all the sliced beetroot in a pan and cover completely with the orange juice, cardamom pods, honey and curry powder. Bring to the boil and simmer for 15 minutes, with a lid on, making sure that the beetroot still has a crunch to it when finished.

Reserve the beetroot by transferring to another dish using a slotted spoon. Turn up the heat and reduce the retained liquid until it is of a thick consistency. Add the garlic, herbs and black pepper. Return the beetroot to the pan to warm through. Drizzle some olive oil over the top before serving.

"My Academy is
my home, my
heart and my life"

The Novel

Resident C

Pappa al Pomodoro
Tomato & Bread Soup

"This dish could be considered the porridge of Tuscany. A simple and easy dish that relies on the freshness of tomato and basil and good olive oil - very little can go wrong!" Felice, resident chef at The Novelli Academy.

Serves: **6-8**
Preparation Time: **5 minutes**
Cooking Time: **15 minutes**
Resting Time: **5 minutes**

Ingredients

225ml extra virgin olive oil
1 small leek (finely chopped)
4 garlic cloves (crushed)
500g tomatoes
(peeled and chopped)
500g stale bread
(torn into small pieces)
1½ ltr vegetable stock
salt and pepper
small bunch fresh basil (chopped)
Parmesan cheese (optional)

Method

Using a large pan, sauté the leeks and garlic, in 75ml of the olive oil for a couple of minutes, or until soft.

Add the tomato and cook for 5-10 minutes. Add the stock, bring to the boil and adjust the seasoning. Add the stale bread.

Cook for 2 minutes then remove from the hob. Cover and leave to rest for at least 30 minutes.

Add the rest of the olive oil and basil, mix well and serve with Parmesan cheese.

Mango na Kelewele
Mango Salad with Plantain Croutons

"This is a simple and refreshing starter, popular in French speaking Africa. I like to use green, unripe mango dressed in lime vinaigrette, sprinkled with spicy plantain croutons." Patti, resident chef at The Novelli Academy.

Serves: **4**
Preparation Time: **15 minutes**
Refrigerate: **60+ minutes**
Cooking Time: **20 minutes**

Ingredients

Green Mango Salad
2 medium, unripe green mangoes
(green and hard to the touch)
2 garlic cloves (crushed)
2 tbsp rapeseed oil
1 lime (juice of)
salt and freshly ground black peppercorns (to season)

Spicy Plantain Croutons
2 fully ripe plantains (yellow)
1 tsp ginger (grated)
2 tbsp rapeseed oil
chilli flakes and salt (to season)
flat-leaf parsley (to garnish)

Chef's Tip

Select a hard mango for this salad, if it gives when squeezed it's too ripe.

The plantain should be ripe - that is when the skin is yellow with a few black markings. The flesh will be a yellowy-orange.

Method

Plantains are one of those exotic foods that are spreading rapidly into Europe and can be found in many high street supermarkets and most Afro-Caribbean and Asian food shops. They are a truly versatile ingredient and have different uses for each stage of their ripeness.
From chips-for-dips when they are green, through to sweet puddings when the skins have turned black.

Plantains are gluten free, high in vitamins A and C, potassium and iron.

If you enjoy curries they also work as a refreshing and palate cleansing side dish.

For The Green Mango Salad
Peel the mango, slice and cut into thin strips and place in a bowl. Mix the garlic, oil and lime juice together then season. Pour over the mango and toss to combine. Cover with clingfilm and refrigerate for 1 hour.

Spicy Plantain Croutons
Preheat the oven to 180ºC (fan), 200ºC (non-fan), gas mark 6.

Peel the plantain and slice lengthways. Cut into cubes and place in a bowl. Add the remaining ingredients and mix to coat the cubes evenly.

Arrange on a baking tray and cook for 20 minutes, or until the plantain is caramelised and golden.

Serve hot with the green mango salad. Garnish with flat-leaf parsley.

Grilled Indian Seekh Kebabs by Manju Malhi

"There are countless recipes for the traditional Seekh kebab and each cook adds their own ingredients to give it a unique flavour. This version uses a paste made from fried onions for a touch of northern Indian sweetness which reflects my father's roots." Manju Malhi, resident chef at The Novelli Academy.

Serves: **4**
Preparation Time: **15 minutes**
Cooking Time: **30 minutes**

Ingredients

Seekh Kebabs
500g minced lamb
1 tbsp malt vinegar
2 tbsp root ginger (peeled and grated)
2 tbsp sunflower or olive oil
2 medium onions (chopped)
½ tsp chilli powder
1 tsp garam masala
2 green chilli peppers (finely chopped keeping the seeds)
2 tbsp gram flour or besan
½ tsp salt
1 medium free range egg (beaten)
oil (for basting)

Mint Chutney
100g coriander leaves (chopped)
30g mint leaves (torn)
2 green chillies (coarsely chopped)
½ tsp salt
1 tsp sugar
1 small onion (roughly chopped)
1 clove garlic
1 tsp root ginger (peeled and grated)

Method

For The Seekh Kebabs
You will need 12 skewers. Mix the minced lamb, in a bowl, with the vinegar and ginger then set aside. Heat the oil in a frying pan, on a medium heat, and add the onions. Fry the onions for about 15 minutes until they are caramelised. Remove and cool the onions then blend them to make a paste. Tip in the chilli powder, garam masala and green chilli peppers then combine. Remove the onion paste mixture from the blender and add to the bowl of minced lamb. Knead for a few minutes to allow all the ingredients to bind well. Just before cooking, add the flour, salt and egg. Mix thoroughly.

With slightly wet hands, mould the meat into long sausage shapes then wind each sausage around the skewers, pressing gently. Brush with a little extra oil and grill under a medium heat, or on the barbecue turning them once, until the meat is cooked right through.

For The Mint Chutney
Place all the ingredients in a blender together with 3-4 tablespoons of water and combine to form a thick paste. This chutney should be consumed on the same day.

Serve the kebab with the mint chutney. Enjoy!

Chef's Tip

Mix the chutney with 1 tablespoon of natural unsweetened yoghurt to make a mint raita.

"I always keep my herbs in ice cold water until the very last moment before they are used."

Accomp

agnements
Sides

Aligot
Traditional French Creamed Potatoes with Cheese & Garlic

19th Century Aubrac monks used bread instead of potatoes for a similar recipe due to a bad harvest.

Serves: **4**
Preparation Time: **10 minutes**
Plus 30 minutes to chill cheese
Cooking Time: **50 minutes**

Ingredients

1kg large potatoes (unpeeled)
75g very mature Cheddar, Comté, or any other strong hard cheese (grated and kept in fridge for 30 minutes)
nutmeg (pinch of)
½ tsp honey
½ tsp mild curry powder
75g unsalted butter (hot, melted)
1 garlic clove per potato (slightly crushed)
75g crème fraîche (warmed)

Chef's Tip

I can't express enough the need to dry the potatoes thoroughly, otherwise the mash will become very watery. Good quality cheese also makes this dish truly exquisite. Adding a sprinkling of smoked paprika before the last stage in the oven helps to glaze the potatoes even more.

Method

Preheat the oven to 140ºC (fan), 160ºC (non-fan), or gas mark 3.

For The Potatoes
In a deep pan, heat plenty of water, enough to cover all the potatoes and bring to the boil. Place all the unpeeled potatoes into the pan and simmer for 20 minutes. Remove and drain in a colander. When cool enough, slice a little off each potato base. Using a spoon, carefully remove the flesh of the potatoes and put this into a mixing bowl. Then add the cheese, nutmeg, honey, curry powder, butter, garlic and warmed crème fraîche. Stir thoroughly and then carefully place the mixture back into the potato skins. Put onto a baking tray. Place in the oven for 30 minutes.

Best served with a freshly grilled steak and some green vegetables.

Carottes Braisées avec Jus d'Orange et Cumin
Carrots Glazed with Orange Juice & Cumin

Introduced to France by Arabic settlers in 1000-1100 AD using some of the many exotic spices brought to Europe from the Middle East.

Serves: **4**
Preparation Time: **5 minutes**
Cooking Time: **30 minutes**

Ingredients

500g fresh baby carrots
(Chantenay or similar, washed, stalks off and unpeeled)
500ml orange juice
(freshly squeezed)
4-5 cardamom pods
1 tsp cumin seeds
½ tsp brown sugar (if the orange juice is acidic and not sweet)
1 tbsp fresh tarragon
1 tbsp extra virgin rapeseed oil (optional)
1 tsp cornflour (optional)

Chef's Tip

As most of the vitamins in carrots are found in the peel, using them unpeeled ensures this healthy goodness is not wasted.

Method

For The Carrots
Warm the carrots in a hot pan, with a lid, with enough orange juice to cover. Add the cardamom pods, the cumin seeds and the sugar, if required. Bring to the boil and allow to simmer until the carrots are cooked - this will depend on how large the carrots are and how you prefer them cooked. Now remove the carrots with a slotted spoon and retain the liquid.

For The Sauce
Increase the heat a little to reduce the liquid slowly. If time is of the essence, mix a tablespoon of juice with a teaspoon of cornflour and return to the pan. Add the tarragon to the thickened sauce.

To Serve
Place the carrots in a serving dish and drizzle with the rapeseed oil. Cover with the sauce and serve.

A perfect accompaniment for fish, meat or other vegetables.

Carottes Râpées
Carrot Salad with
Pine Kernels

A popular dish in France due to carrots being grown in most regions across the country throughout the year.

Serves: **4**
Preparation Time: **35 minutes**
Plus 3 hours in fridge
Cooking Time: **30 minutes**

Ingredients

500g carrots (washed, grated and kept in fridge until required)
1 passion fruit (sliced in half and the flesh removed and kept)
2 oranges (juiced)
½ vanilla pod (sliced in half lengthways)
5 cardamom pods
½ tsp mustard seeds
1 sprig thyme
2 tsp Acacia honey
3 tbsp extra virgin olive oil
2 garlic cloves (crushed)
2 tsp chervil (chopped)
1 tbsp chives (chopped)
100g pine kernels
seasoning as required

Chef's Tip

Keep the carrots in the fridge until the very last moment. This will ensure crispness, which is very important for this recipe.

Method

For The Carrots
Mix the chilled grated carrots and passion fruit flesh together in a mixing bowl, then place in the fridge for up to 3 hours.

For The Salad Dressing
Using a pan on a medium heat, reduce the orange juice to half its quantity. Add the vanilla pod, cardamom pods and thyme and continue reducing for a further 10 minutes. Turn off the heat and, when cool, place in the fridge. This is your salad dressing.

To Prepare
In a dry frying pan, lightly toast the pine kernels. Remove from the pan and keep to one side.

Remove the grated carrot mix from the fridge. Strain the juice that has been naturally created in the fridge into another bowl. Then, add the crushed garlic, mustard seeds, crushed black pepper, honey and extra virgin olive oil and mix thoroughly into the carrots.

Mix the juice strained from the carrots with a little of the reduced orange dressing.

To Serve
Add some of the orange juice dressing to the carrot mixture and mix thoroughly. Arrange in a clean serving bowl or on a plate with a large spoon. Drizzle the rest of the reduced orange juice dressing over the carrots. Sprinkle with the green chopped herbs and pine kernels. Enjoy!

Chou Vert aux Lardons Fumés
Savoy Cabbage with Smoked Bacon

This is a dish I created using some of the most flavoursome, exciting spices and healthy ingredients.

Serves: **4**
Preparation Time: **20 minutes**
Cooking Time: **10 minutes**

Ingredients

1 Savoy cabbage (whole)
2 tbsp extra virgin rapeseed oil
150g smoked lardons (small dice)
2 garlic cloves (roughly crushed)
½ tsp mild curry powder
1 tsp caraway seeds
1 tsp celery seeds
3 tbsp crème fraîche
crushed black pepper (to taste)

Chef's Tip

At certain times of the year cabbage can be a little lacking in taste. I recommend using vegetable stock to boil the cabbage, rather than water as this will add flavour.

Method

For The Cabbage

Cut the cabbage in half. Remove any dry leaves and the stalk.

Heat a large pan of water to boiling point. Plunge the cabbage halves into a large pan of steadily boiling water (or stock - see tip). Boil for 2 minutes and then drain for 15 minutes using a colander over a bowl. Cut each half of the cabbage into halves and half again making a total of 8 pieces.

For The Smoked Lardons

Return the same empty pan to a high heat. Add the rapeseed oil, diced lardons and the garlic cloves - which have been roughly crushed with the edge of your kitchen knife, or smashed with your hand on the board. Sauté for 2 minutes on a high heat. Then, add the curry powder, the caraway and celery seeds and the crushed black pepper, as required. Mix well. Next, add the 8 pieces of cabbage and stir carefully into the mixture. Cover, then sauté for a further 5-10 minutes - don't worry if your 8 pieces of cabbage separate, this is normal! Check the seasoning again, then stir in the crème fraîche and heat for approx 1 minute. Now you can serve this beautiful side dish.

94

Courgette à la Tante Helga
Courgettes Cooked Aunty Helga's Way

My very good friend Helga ('aunty' to the kids) makes this dish for us when we visit her in her beautiful home in Austria.

Serves: **4**
Preparation Time: **5 minutes**
Cooking Time: **15 minutes**

Ingredients

3 shallots (chopped)
½ tsp fennel seeds
½ tsp cumin seeds
1 tbsp rapeseed oil
4 plum tomatoes
1 sprig thyme
2 bay leaves
2 garlic cloves (crushed)
3 large courgettes (roughly chopped)
½ tsp paprika
handful of basil and parsley (torn)
80g Beaufort or Comté cheese (grated)
cracked black pepper (to taste)

Gasteinertal, Austria

Chef's Tip

Adding the cheese at the very end ensures that all of the full flavours are retained.

Method

In a sauté pan, with a lid, sweat the shallots with the fennel and cumin and the rapeseed oil for 5 minutes. Do not colour. Whilst sweating, roll the tomatoes carefully on a hard surface before quartering and adding to the pan, making sure you catch all the juice that will now pour out. Then, heat and cover for 2 minutes. Add the thyme, garlic and bay leaves followed by the courgettes.

Place the lid on the pan and steam for 10 minutes. Add the paprika and stir thoroughly followed by the torn basil and parsley. Add the cheese and stir once. Remove from the heat. Serve immediately.

Gratin de Chou-Fleur
Cauliflower Gratin

Originated in the Middle East, this dish has been very popular in Britain since Louis XV reigned in France.

Serves: **4-6**
Preparation Time: **10 minutes**
Cooking Time: **70 minutes**

Ingredients

1 large cauliflower (whole, green leaves removed and washed)
semi-skimmed milk (enough to cover)
½ tsp grated nutmeg
2 bay leaves
1 garlic bulb (halved)
1 sprig thyme
crushed black pepper (to taste)
sugar (pinch of)

For The Sauce
250-300ml milk used to cook the cauliflower
1 tbsp plain flour
1 tbsp rapeseed oil (for the roux)
100g Beaufort/Gruyère type cheese (cubed and kept cold)

For The Persillade
75g breadcrumbs
3 cloves garlic (crushed)
60-70g green herbs (parsley, basil, chervil, thyme flowers - finely chopped)

Chef's Tip

This can be prepared in advance and cooked from room temperature shortly before serving.

Method

Preheat the oven to 140ºC (fan), 160ºC (non-fan), or gas mark 3.

To Cook The Cauliflower
Place the cauliflower into a large pan and cover with milk, enough to cover completely. Add the nutmeg, bay leaves, halved garlic, sprig of thyme, black pepper and sugar. Bring to a simmer and cook, covered, for 20 minutes. Remove the cauliflower and place on a baking tray, retaining the milk. Place the cauliflower into the preheated oven for approx 30 minutes to help dry it out. The smell from the kitchen at this stage will be amazing!

To Make The Sauce
Strain the milk used to cook the cauliflower. In another pan, add the flour and rapeseed oil and mix with a wooden spoon to create a roux paste. Add approx 250-300ml of the strained milk and stir continuously over a medium heat until it thickens. Add the cold, cubed cheese and remove from the heat. Stir whilst off the heat.

For The Persillade
Thoroughly combine the breadcrumbs, herbs and garlic.

To Prepare Before Serving
Take the cauliflower out of the oven and place in another baking pan. Cover with the béchamel sauce (cheese sauce) and then the Persillade. Place in the oven shortly before serving for 12 minutes on a high heat - 180ºC (fan), 200ºC (non-fan), or gas mark 6 until the breadcrumb topping is golden brown.

Serve immediately.

99

Tartiflette
Creamy Oven Baked Sweet Potatoes with Bacon

This recipe nearly always uses Reblochon cheese to give it its true flavour. It is difficult to reduce the fat content without losing the taste.

Serves: **4**
Preparation Time: **30 minutes**
Cooking Time: **45 minutes**

Ingredients

100ml full-fat milk
100ml single cream
2 bay leaves
1 tsp cumin seeds
700g sweet potatoes (unpeeled and sliced in ½cm large slices)
8 rashers thick cut, smoked bacon (cut into 2cm pieces)
1 onion (sliced)
1 sprig thyme
2 garlic cloves (crushed)
300g Reblochon cheese (cubed and kept very cold)
1 tbsp mustard seeds (or Dijon/English mustard)
crushed black pepper

Method

Preheat the oven to 200ºC (fan), 220ºC (non-fan), or gas mark 7.

For The Cheese Sauce
Bring the milk to the boil in a milk pan and simmer for 2 minutes. Add the cream and simmer again for 2 minutes. Add the bay leaves, cumin seeds and mustard. Turn off the heat. Whilst cooling, add the cheese but DO NOT stir - simply leave to infuse and cover with a lid.

For The Sweet Potatoes
In a separate, very hot, large sauté pan, with a lid, fry the bacon - with no oil. Grind some freshly cracked black pepper over the bacon and allow to colour. Add the onions, garlic and thyme, then cover with the lid. When the onions start to soften, add the sliced potatoes. Mix and turn the heat down. Cook for 10 minutes. Remove from the heat until required.

To Assemble
Using an ovenproof dish, layer the potatoes, warm the cheese sauce a little and cover the potatoes. Bake for 25 minutes and serve hot. Delicious!

Chef's Tip

The components of this dish can be prepared in advance. Make sure everything is at room temperature before assembling. Various potatoes can be used, including unusual types like Belle de Fontenay. The single cream can be exchanged for crème fraîche and the milk to semi-skimmed to reduce the fat content but the full rich flavour may be compromised.

Aioli
Garlic Mayonnaise

First created to accompany fish dishes, it originated in the Languedoc region of France and Catalonian region of northern Spain.

Makes: **500ml**
Preparation Time: **15 minutes**

Ingredients

1 garlic bulb (peeled and crushed)
3 egg yolks
500ml extra virgin olive oil
1 lemon (juice of)
8 basil leaves
(kept in ice cold water to keep fresh)
ground black pepper (to taste)
1 tsp honey (only if not using the infused oil - see chef's tip below)

Chef's Tip

Instead of using extra virgin olive oil, try using my tomato and vanilla infused olive oil (see recipe page 106). I find this adds extra flavour and also a magnificent colour.

Method

To Crush The Garlic
Place some of the garlic in a pestle and mortar and start pounding the garlic. Gradually add more garlic until a nice smooth paste forms.

For The Mayonnaise
In a separate mixing bowl, whisk the egg yolks. Once they are nice and creamy, start adding the olive oil, a slow drizzle to start with. Whisk vigorously, then add the remaining oil and whisk until the sauce becomes an emulsion and is smooth and thick in texture. Finely tear the basil, then add. Grind a little black pepper to taste, add the garlic paste and stir everything together. Add the honey (if using) and lemon juice.

Fill a Kilner jar with the aioli and keep in the fridge for up to 5 days. This will depend on how fresh your ingredients were to start with.

Aioli can be used as an accompaniment to several different dishes, or just a dip with fresh bread as an appetiser.

Huile d'Infusion de Tomate et Vanille
Tomato & Vanilla Infused Oil

This is my own creation and I use it to enhance the flavours in particular recipes.

Makes: **Approx 500ml**
Preparation Time: **10 minutes**
Plus at least 60 minutes to infuse

Ingredients

1kg plum tomatoes
(core removed and diced)
1 tsp smoked paprika
½ vanilla pod (sliced lengthways)
1 tbsp tomato purée
ground black pepper
10 basil leaves
2 tsp honey
400ml extra virgin olive oil
½ lemon (juice of)
3 garlic cloves (crushed)

Chef's Tip

You can try this recipe by substituting all the tomatoes for chopped red peppers and adding thyme, bay leaves and cumin seeds into the pulped mixture before adding the oil. Extra virgin rapeseed oil can also be used for a slightly healthier version.

Method

For The Tomatoes
Heat all the diced tomatoes gently in a pan until they reduce a little. Add the honey, paprika, tomato purée, vanilla, basil leaves and continue to reduce slowly. Once the consistency resembles a tomato pulp, add the crushed garlic and set aside.

To Infuse
The next part of the recipe is very important for the best results. DO NOT STIR the following. Add the olive oil to the tomato pulp and swirl the pan gently, but DO NOT STIR! Cover with a lid and leave to infuse for a minimum of 1 hour.

To Finish
Using a fine sieve or even a coffee filter, strain the contents of the pan into another bowl and add a squeeze of lemon. The oil can then be stored in a Kilner jar for up to 2 weeks and used in many ways.

The residue tomato pulp, left in the sieve, can be used as a base for dipping bread into, pasta sauces, pizza bases and can be thinned slightly using either hot stock or hot water.

Sauce Nantua
Crayfish Sauce

Named after the town of Nantua near Lyon, this sauce is typically made with crayfish and is a great accompaniment for many fish based recipes.

Serves: **As required**
Preparation Time: **10 minutes**
Cooking Time: **40 minutes**

Ingredients

2 tbsp extra virgin rapeseed oil
2 sticks celery (diced)
2 onions (diced)
2 carrots (diced)
15 crayfish (flesh removed from shells and kept separately)
1 clove garlic (crushed)
1 tsp Cognac
10g cornflour
(mixed with 1 tbsp cold water)
10ml dry white wine
6 plum tomatoes (diced)
2 tbsp tomato purée
1 tsp honey
750ml hot, strong fish stock
cayenne pepper (pinch of)
1 sprig thyme
1 bay leaf
2 tbsp extra virgin olive oil
1 tbsp chopped green herbs
(eg basil, parsley, chervil or tarragon)
2 tbsp crème fraîche

Method

Heat the rapeseed oil in a hot, deep pan. Sweat the celery, onions and carrots slowly for about 10 minutes. Add the garlic, crayfish shells (chopped) and Cognac and carefully flambé. When the flames have dispersed, add the cornflour mix, tomatoes, honey, tomato purée and white wine, cayenne pepper, sprig of thyme, bay leaf and bring to the boil. Simmer for 5 minutes and add the hot stock. Simmer uncovered for 40 minutes.

Pass everything through a mouli or a fine sieve (chinois) and add the chopped green herbs to the sauce with the extra virgin olive oil. Stir in the crème fraîche and add the crayfish meat which will cook it immediately.

Chef's Tip

This sauce can be poured over any fish to give a wonderful rich taste. Simply bake in the oven at 160ºC (fan) and serve after about 10 minutes.

Sauce de Tomate Piquante
Tomato Chilli Sauce

I use tomatoes in many recipes and found that I needed to help intensify the flavour at certain times of the year when tomatoes aren't so tasty. Et voila!

Serves: **As required**
Preparation Time: **10 minutes**
Cooking Time: **40 minutes**

Ingredients

450g cherry tomatoes (halved)
2 tbsp groundnut oil
50g pitted prunes
(pulped to a purée)
200g red onions (sliced)
1 tbsp grenadine (optional)
1 bird's eye chilli (finely sliced)
2 tsp coriander seeds
½ garlic bulb (peeled and crushed)
½ vanilla pod
1 star anise
50g fresh ginger (grated)
½ tsp smoked paprika
130g honey
150ml sherry vinegar

Chef's Tip

Using a good quality smoked paprika will add to the flavours and I think I have found the best, La Chinata!

Method

Make sure you are using a sauté pan with a lid.

Cut the tomatoes in half and place them into a hot sauté pan (without any oil) and uncovered. This will help to evaporate the moisture held within the tomatoes. After about 10-15 minutes the tomatoes should reduce to a brightly coloured concentrate. Remove from the pan carefully and keep to one side.

Using the same pan, which is now back on a moderate heat, add the groundnut oil, puréed prunes, onions, grenadine (if using), chilli, coriander seeds, garlic, vanilla, star anise, ginger and smoked paprika and stir carefully. After approx 5 minutes of simmering, the mixture should have the consistency of syrup. Add the honey and vinegar then stir. Re-introduce the tomatoes and stir carefully once. Cover with the lid and allow to simmer for 20 minutes, occasionally stirring gently.

Once cooled, spoon the tomato sauce into jars and keep in the fridge for up to 7 days. Use as required.

Tapenade
Black Olive & Anchovy Paste

Tapenade comes from the Provençale word for capers, 'tapenas'. It is traditionally used as a spread for bread and served as an hors d'oeuvre.

Serves: **As required**
Preparation Time: **10 minutes**

Ingredients

200g pitted black olives
5 anchovy fillets
2 tbsp capers
1 garlic bulb
(peeled and crushed cloves)
½ tsp honey
1 tsp Dijon mustard
crushed black pepper (to taste)
10ml extra virgin olive oil
(warmed slightly)
10 fresh basil leaves

Chef's Tip

Using good quality olives will help infuse and improve the taste of the tapenade.

Method

Combine all the ingredients apart from the olive oil and basil leaves. You can use a mixing bowl and a hand blender, a liquidiser or a pestle and mortar. Grind everything into a smooth paste then gradually add the warm oil and the basil leaves. Spoon the smooth mixture into a kilner jar and keep in the fridge.

The tapenade should keep for up to 7 days in the fridge.

Vinaigrette de Maman Novelli
My Mother's Basic Vinaigrette

This vinaigrette is something my mother always makes and keeps in jars and simply tops up the liquid as she uses it.

Serves: **As required**
Preparation Time: **10 minutes**

Ingredients

2 garlic cloves (crushed)
2 shallots (finely diced)
2 tsp mustard (French or English)
2 tbsp sherry vinegar or mature balsamic vinegar
cold pressed extra virgin olive oil
hot water
crushed black pepper and a sprinkle of salt
1 sprig rosemary
1 sprig thyme

1 large Kilner-type jar

Chef's Tip

This can be made in advance and kept in the fridge. It can be used on the usual avocado, salads and tomatoes but also tastes great drizzled over cold meats and fish.

Method

Mix all of the ingredients, except the oil and hot water, and place in a Kilner jar. Then, fill the jar with a combination of oil and boiling water (from the kettle) - the quantities will differ depending on the size of your jar. Follow a ratio of one part oil to two parts water. Seal the lid and, once cooled, place into the fridge for a minimum of 20 minutes. Do not open the lid until the contents are completely cold.

Use as required.

Plats

Principaux
Mains

"I use extra virgin rapeseed oil when I'm cooking. It's high in Omega 3 and has much less saturated fat than olive oil."

Bouillabaisse Mediterranean Fish Stew

Serves: **4**
Preparation Time: **30 minutes**
Cooking Time: **75 minutes**

Ingredients

1kg of 4 different fish
(eg gurnard, hake, cod, prawns or
haddock left on the bone)
2 tbsp extra virgin rapeseed oil
2 onions (diced)
2 carrots (diced)
1 red pepper (diced)
1 bulb fennel (diced)
2 sticks celery (diced)
1 leek (sliced)
1 red chilli (finely sliced)
6 plum tomatoes (chopped)
2 bay leaves
1 sprig rosemary
1 sprig thyme
½ bulb garlic
2 tbsp tomato purée
4 anchovy fillets (chopped)
1 tsp honey
½ tsp Spanish saffron
1 orange (juice and peel)
water or fish stock (to cover)
6 small new potatoes (halved)
200g Gruyère cheese (grated)
2 tbsp extra virgin olive oil
1 sprig fresh basil leaves

Method

Preheat the oven to 180°C (fan), 200°C (non-fan),
or gas mark 6.

Filleting The Fish
When buying your fish, ask the fishmonger to fillet it and to
give you all the bones and off-cuts separately. If this isn't
possible, fillet the fish yourself. Place the fish flat on a
board and start at the head end. Using a flexible, filleting
knife, place the knife behind the gills, make an incision
towards the head but not through the fish. Twist the knife
so that the blade is facing the tail and carefully use the
knife to cut towards the tail, holding the fish in one place.
That should leave you with one slice of fish with only the
skin left on. Pick out any bones that are visible and repeat
the process for the other side of the fish.

Chef's Tip

Using good quality fresh fish with good quality fish stock will help improve the flavours of this dish.

This recipe originated in Marseille where fishermen would start the stew in the morning, with their catch of the day, and eat it later in the afternoon. This technique goes back to the ancient Greek times around the 7th Century.

To Prepare The Fish

Heat the rapeseed oil in a large, deep, hot pan, with a lid, and panfry all the fillets, skin-side down for 2 minutes. Remove and set aside.

For The Soup

The remaining fish parts need to be chopped and placed into the same pan that the fillets were fried in. Add all the diced vegetables (except the potatoes), plum tomatoes, the herbs (except the basil), chilli and the garlic and sweat. After about 5 minutes of sweating, add the tomato purée, honey, anchovies, saffron, the juice of the orange along with the orange peel and water or fish stock to cover. Bring to the boil and simmer for 40 minutes, skimming off the impurities every 10 minutes.

For The Potatoes

Add the potatoes to the pan and cook for a further 20 minutes. Then, remove the potatoes, one by one, and reserve with the fish fillets.

Pass all the remaining contents of the pan through a mouli (if available) or blend with a hand blender and pass through a fine mesh conical sieve (chinois).

To Warm The Fish

Return the strained liquid to a clean pan and bring to the boil. Taste and adjust the seasoning to suit you, then add the fish fillets to warm through.

To Serve

Place the potatoes on a baking tray and cover with the grated Gruyère cheese. Place into the oven for 5 minutes before serving.

In a bowl, add the extra virgin olive oil and the freshly washed basil and allow to infuse for a few minutes.

Place the fish fillets into a large serving bowl (or smaller individual bowls) and cover with the soup. Add the cheese covered potatoes, then drizzle over some of the infused oil.

Cabillaud au Jus de Pomme
Loin of Cod with Apple Juice Reduction

This dish was inspired by trips to Normandy when I was a young man and the various dishes that can be made using such a versatile fruit like the apple.

Serves: **4**
Preparation Time: **10 minutes**
Cooking Time: **40 minutes**

Ingredients

4 x 175g cod loin
2 tbsp extra virgin rapeseed oil
1 tsp curry powder
1 tsp cumin seeds
7 shallots (finely sliced)
few sprigs thyme
a little ground black pepper
(to taste)
2 cloves garlic (crushed)
120ml dry apple juice
1 tbsp flat-leaf parsley (chopped)
1 tbsp tarragon (chopped)
3 tbsp extra virgin olive oil
(or extra virgin rapeseed oil)
1 tbsp mustard seeds
(or wholegrain mustard)
200g crème fraîche
1 tsp honey

Chef's Tip

Use good quality, freshly pressed apple juice as the sugar content will help create a better tasting sauce.

Method

For The Cod

Preheat a heavy based pan, with a lid. Heat the rapeseed oil with the curry powder and cumin seeds. Stir the spices and place the cod into the pan, skin-side down.

Add half of the prepared shallots into the pan, then add the thyme, black pepper and crushed garlic.

Turn the fish over and cover with a tight fitting lid - making sure the pan is very hot. Heat for about 5 minutes, then pour in 60ml of the apple juice. Once the juices have reduced, which shouldn't take longer than 5 minutes, remove the fish from the pan along with the shallots. Transfer to a plate and cover with clingfilm.

To Prepare The Sauce

Sprinkle the chopped parsley and tarragon over the remaining shallots and leave to infuse with the olive oil in a sauté pan, then pour the remaining apple juice into the pan and heat gently. Stir in the mustard. Drain the fish juices from the plate and add these to the pan. Reduce the cooking liquor by half, stirring in the crème fraîche and the honey once the reduction is nice and thick (so that it coats the back of a spoon).

Return the fish back to the hot pan. The dish looks and smells fantastic served hot, straight from the pan.

Cassoulet de Cabillaud
Cassoulet of Cod

Popular in the Languedoc and Midi-Pyrénées regions of France. White beans are used as a base for this wonderful dish.

Serves: **4**
Preparation Time: **30 minutes**
Soak the beans the overnight
Cooking Time: **60 minutes**

Ingredients

600g cod fillets
300g white beans (soaked overnight)
3 onions (sliced)
3 cloves garlic (crushed)
150g smoked pancetta (sliced)
or lardons
4 tomatoes (chopped)
1 tbsp rosemary
1 tsp honey
1 tsp white wine vinegar
250ml dry white wine
1 tbsp tomato purée
100g white breadcrumbs
(toasted in a dry pan)
100g Parmesan cheese
(finely grated)
1 tbsp parsley (chopped)
80ml extra virgin olive oil

Chef's Tip

Fresh fish is a very important part of this recipe as the fresher the fish, the better the flavours.

Method

To Prepare The Beans
Soak the beans in water overnight or in warm water for up to 3 hours. Strain and keep to one side.

For The Cassoulet
Sweat the onions, garlic, pancetta, tomatoes and rosemary for about 10 minutes in a hot, large sauté pan. Add the honey and vinegar. Reduce the liquid a little, then add the white wine, tomato purée and the soaked beans. Simmer, covered, for 40 minutes then place the cod into the pan, skin-side down. Continue simmering, with the lid on, for a further 10 minutes. Place to one side.

For The Parmesan Crumb
In a separate bowl, mix the Parmesan cheese, toasted breadcrumbs and chopped parsley with the olive oil and stir thoroughly.

To Serve
Spoon the Parmesan mixture over the fish and bean mixture. Place under a hot grill until the cheese starts to change colour. Serve immediately.

Galettes d'Églefin Fumé Smoked Haddock & Sweet Potato Bake

This dish is popular in the north west of France near the Atlantic coast where haddock is plentiful.

Serves: **4**
Preparation Time: **10 minutes**
Cooking Time: **50 minutes**

Ingredients

250g smoked haddock
600g sweet potatoes (unpeeled)
200g Rustique or good quality Camembert cheese (cubed)
1 large onion (sliced)
2 eggs (beaten in a bowl)
½ tsp cayenne pepper or chilli powder
½ tsp turmeric
1 sprig thyme
crushed black pepper (to taste)
2 cloves garlic (crushed)
50g white breadcrumbs (lightly toasted)
1 tbsp parsley (finely chopped)

crisp green salad (to serve)

Chef's Tip

This recipe can be made in advance. Just remember to warm the galette from room temperature in the oven for about 20 minutes before grilling.

Method

Preheat the oven to 180ºC (fan), 200ºC (non-fan), or gas mark 6.

Arrange the sweet potatoes on a baking tray and place into the hot oven for approx 30-40 minutes.

In a medium hot pan, with a lid, sweat the onions slowly with the crushed pepper, thyme and garlic. When the onions are soft, but not brown, flake the fish into the pan. Stir, then cover and continue to heat through with the lid on for approx 5 minutes. The smoked haddock doesn't need too much cooking as it is already smoked. If you cook it for too long the fish will become tough and chewy.

Once the potatoes are baked, cut lengthways and scoop out the mash. Place into a mixing bowl. Introduce the egg into the mash slowly, then the onions with the fish. Add the remaining ingredients, mix and place in a lightly fingertip-oiled pie dish. Sprinkle over the breadcrumbs mixed with the parsley and place under a grill for about 10 minutes or until golden brown and slightly firm to the touch. Serve immediately.

Delicious with a green crispy salad.

Lotte Provençale
Monkfish with Tomatoes, Herbs & Garlic

This popular dish from the south of France has been enjoyed for many years, since fishermen discovered that the flesh from such an ugly fish was so tasty!

Serves: **4**
Preparation Time: **15 minutes**
Cooking Time: **20 minutes**

Ingredients

1kg fresh cleaned monkfish
(or any other firm, fresh fish fillet eg cod, halibut, haddock, hake)
1 tbsp extra virgin rapeseed oil
2 onions (finely sliced)
½ fennel bulb (finely sliced)
1 yellow pepper (diced)
1 tsp smoked paprika
1 sprig thyme
4 leaves sage
10 black olives
1 tsp honey
2 cloves garlic (crushed)
400g chopped tinned tomatoes
(or 6 unpeeled plum tomatoes, diced)
125ml dry white wine and vegetable stock (mixed 50-50)
1 bunch fresh basil
(kept in ice cold water)
2 tbsp extra virgin olive oil

Method

In a large sauté pan, heat the rapeseed oil and introduce the fish. Fry on each side for approx 5 minutes. Take the fish out carefully and place on a plate. Cover with clingfilm.

In the same pan, add the onions, fennel, pepper, smoked paprika, thyme, sage, olives, honey, garlic and tomatoes. Sweat until everything is soft - approx 10 minutes. Then add the stock and wine (if using) and simmer for a further 10 minutes uncovered.

Just before serving, place the fish back into the pan until warmed through. Tear some of the wet, fresh basil leaves and sprinkle over the pan. Drizzle the olive oil over the dish to give a little shine to the fish and vegetables. Serve in the pan.

Chef's Tip

If you have been able to remove the skin before cooking, great, but if using a fish with the skin on, initially fry the fish skin-side down and then, when you have turned the fish over to fry the other side, gently remove the skin to serve.

Keeping any herbs in ice cold water helps to increase the intensity of the herb and improves aromas.

Morue à la Catalane
Cod Catalan Style

This dish originates from the Catalan region that borders France and northern Spain.

Serves: **4**
Preparation Time: **15 minutes**
Cooking Time: **25 minutes**

Ingredients

4 cod fillets (skin on)
700g plum tomatoes (chopped)
3 shallots (chopped)
½ bulb garlic
1 sprig rosemary
1 sprig thyme
2 bay leaves
1 tbsp parsley and fresh basil (chopped)
2 tbsp extra virgin olive oil
10 black olives
cracked black pepper
2 tbsp extra virgin rapeseed oil (for frying)

crispy salad and steamed rice (to serve)

Chef's Tip

Any good quality, firm fish can be used for this dish, especially one of my favourites, red snapper.

Method

Preheat the oven to 160°C (fan), 180°C (non-fan), or gas mark 4.

To Prepare The Sauce
Using a blender or liquidiser, blitz the tomatoes and shallots for a few seconds. Transfer this mixture into a sauté pan, with a lid, and bring to the boil. Add the garlic, rosemary, thyme and bay leaves and simmer for 10 minutes to reduce the sauce slightly. Season with black pepper to taste, then add the olives.

For The Fish
In another pan, heat the rapeseed oil. Introduce the fish, skin-side down. Sear for 2 minutes then remove from the heat.

Place the fish in an ovenproof (gratin) dish. Cover with the tomato sauce and bake for 10 minutes.

While the fish is in the oven, mix the fresh herbs with the olive oil and let it infuse.

When the 10 minutes of baking time is finished, drizzle the infused oil over the fish dish and serve. This is perfect with steamed rice and a crispy salad.

Morue Roti à la Sauce Romanesque
Cod with a Marie Rose Style Sauce

Serves: **4**
Preparation Time: **10 minutes**
Cooking Time: **60 minutes**

Ingredients

1kg fresh cod fillets (skin left on)
6 plum tomatoes
1 red pepper (left whole)
1 garlic bulb (halved)
1 onion (sliced)
2 dried nora peppers
(or large dried chillies)
2 tsp smoked paprika
2 sprigs thyme
60g whole almonds (blanched)
2 slices toasted brioche or
toasted bread (broken into pieces)
2 tbsp extra virgin olive oil
1 tbsp extra virgin rapeseed oil
(for frying)
1 tbsp Jerez or sherry vinegar
1 tsp honey
salt and crushed pepper (pinch of)
1 tsp tapenade (see page 112)

Garnish
chervil, chopped parsley,
or micro-cress

Chef's Tip

There is no need to season fresh fish when cooking as the fish has enough natural salt absorbed in its flesh.

Originating from the Nîmes region of southern France, this recipe has Mediterranean and North African influences and is full of flavour.

Method

Preheat the oven to 160°C (fan), 180°C (non-fan), or gas mark 4.

To Make The Sauce

Place a non-stick baking tray, covered with foil, into the preheated oven. Place the tomatoes, pepper, 1 half of the garlic, onions, chilli, paprika and 1 sprig of thyme on the tray. In a corner of the tray, scatter the almonds and bread (away from the juices that will be created). Bake for 30 minutes.

Remove from the oven. When cool enough, peel the garlic, remove the stalk and seeds from the pepper and put all the ingredients into a blender. Add the olive oil, vinegar, honey and all of the juices from the baking tray and blitz until you have a smooth sauce. Place the sauce in a pan, with a lid, and bring to a simmer on the stove. Taste and season as required.

For The Cod

Heat a non-stick frying pan and when hot add the remaining sprig of thyme, the remaining half of the garlic bulb and the rapeseed oil. Place the cod skin-side down for 2 minutes, then turn over and fry for a further 10 minutes with a lid on. Remove from the heat and carefully remove the skin from the fish.

Arrange your cod onto your serving dish and drizzle with Romanesque sauce. Decorate with fresh chervil, chopped parsley or micro-cress and tapenade.

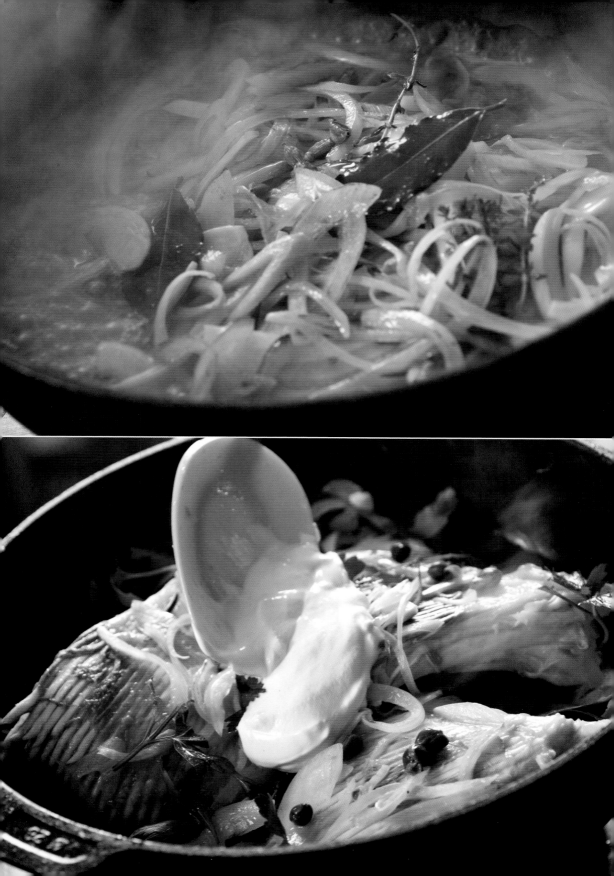

Raie à la Sauce Moutarde
Skate in a Mustard Sauce

This recipe was inspired by my love of skate with black butter and capers, although this goes against all my healthy principles of cooking that I teach in my Academy.

Serves: **4**
Preparation Time: **10 minutes**
Cooking Time: **20 minutes**

Ingredients

2 skate wings (cleaned and prepared by your fishmonger)
1 tbsp extra virgin rapeseed oil
2 shallots (sliced)
½ fennel (sliced)
100ml fish stock (hot)
3 tbsp mustard (French or English)
100ml crème fraîche
1 tbsp capers (chopped)
small bunch flat-leaf parsley (chopped)
2 bay leaves

Chef's Tip

This is a very easy dish to prepare and cook. Ideal if you are in a hurry to create something tasty and quick.

Make sure the skate is very fresh otherwise it will smell of ammonia.

Method

In a deep pan with a lid, heat the oil and sweat the shallots and fennel. Add the hot stock, stir in the mustard and add the bay leaves.

Add the skate and enough stock to cover the fish. Bring to the boil, then reduce to a simmer for 15 minutes.
Remove from the heat and add the crème fraîche, capers and parsley. Serve immediately from the pan.

Waterzooï
Northern French
Mixed Fish Casserole

This is a typical dish from northern France and some parts of Belgium, normally made using fish local to that part of the world.

Serves: **4**
Preparation Time: **20 minutes**
Cooking Time: **15 minutes**

Ingredients

700g mixed fillets of fish
2 tbsp extra virgin rapeseed oil
1 tsp cumin seeds
2 sprigs thyme
(stalks and flowers kept separately)
1 bay leaf
2 carrots (sliced julienne)
¼ celeriac (sliced julienne)
2 sticks celery (sliced julienne)
1 leek (sliced julienne)
½ cucumber (sliced julienne)
1 lemon (juice of)
1ltr hot, strong fish stock
1 tsp cornflour
(blended with 1 tbsp cold water)
250ml double cream
2 tbsp olive oil
1 sprig chervil
1 sprig chives

Method

For The Vegetables
In a deep pan with a lid, heat the oil adding the cumin seeds, thyme flowers (no stalks) and bay leaf and infuse for 2 minutes. Reduce the heat a little and add the carrots and celeriac. Stir for 2 minutes without colouring. Add the celery and leeks and slowly sauté for 1 minute. Finally, add the cucumber and a squeeze of lemon juice and heat for no more than 10 seconds. Strain everything over a bowl and retain the juices for the soup.

To Cook The Fish
Using the same pan, on a medium heat, place the fish fillets, skin-side down, with the thyme stalks and slowly fry without colouring the fish. Spoon the vegetables from the strainer over the fish and remove from the heat.

For The Soup
Heat the fish stock in a deep pan and add the juices from the strained vegetables. Simmer for 10 minutes and reduce by half. If in a hurry, stir in the cornflour to thicken the sauce. Pass the sauce through a fine sieve. When cool, add the cream.

To Serve
Bring the sauce back to the boil and pour over the fish. Serve immediately.

Chef's Tip

Instead of using fish, you could use chicken and change the fish stock to chicken or vegetable stock.

Carbonnade de Chevreuil à la Bière Brune

Venison in a Beer Casserole

This is a northern French version of a normal Carbonnade.

Serves: **4-6**
Preparation Time: **15 minutes**
Cooking Time: **2½ hours**

Ingredients

1kg venison leg (cut into 2cm cubes)
1 tsp crushed black pepper
1 tsp fennel seeds
1 tsp cumin seeds
1 sprig thyme
2 bay leaves
5 leaves sage
1 tbsp sugar
½ tbsp English mustard
375ml stout beer
375ml hot beef stock
½ tbsp course grain mustard
3 whole chicory bulbs
(halved lengthways)
3 large onions (sliced)

Chef's Tip

This dish shouldn't need any extra fat or salt as the herbs, spices and cooking techniques help to keep it flavoursome but healthy.

Method

Preheat the oven to 140ºC (fan), 160ºC (non-fan), or gas mark 3.

Sauté the venison cubes quickly in oil to seal on all sides using a very hot sauté pan with a lid. Add a little water and cover with the lid for 10-15 minutes. Remove the venison and drain. Discard the juices (fat) from the pan.

Return the pan to the heat with the venison. Add the black pepper, fennel seeds, cumin, thyme, bay leaves, sage, onions, sugar, English mustard, beer and stock to cover the venison. Bring to the boil, then reduce to a simmer. After approx 15 minutes, skim the impurities from the top of the stock. Cover and place the pan into the oven for 1½ hours.

Taste the sauce for flavour and adjust any seasoning. Add the chicory leaves, having discarded the dry outside leaves. Cover and place back in the oven for a further 30-45 minutes, depending on the quality of the venison. Remove from the oven.

Taste the sauce again, and if the chicory has made the sauce a little acidic, add a little more sugar and the course grain mustard, stir into the sauce and taste once again.

Serve from the pan.

Lapin Chasseur
Rabbit Casserole

Chasseur sauce is reputed to have been created by 16th Century diplomat and French cuisine pioneer Philippe de Mornay, as an accompaniment to various game dishes.

Serves: **4**
Preparation Time: **15 minutes**
Cooking Time: **60 minutes**

Ingredients

1 rabbit
(skin removed and cut into 8 pieces)
2 tbsp extra virgin rapeseed oil
1 onion (sliced)
1 sprig thyme
(stalk and leaves separated)
1 bulb garlic
(halved widthways, unpeeled)
crushed black pepper (to taste)
50ml Cognac
2 tbsp honey
½ tsp cayenne pepper
1½ tbsp cornflour
150g smoked lardons (diced)
2 plum tomatoes (quartered)
100ml white wine
½ Portobello mushroom
(or 2 chestnut mushrooms)
2 tbsp crème fraîche
2 tbsp extra virgin olive oil
1 sprig tarragon
1 lemon (juice of)

Method

Preheat the oven to 160ºC (fan), 180º (non-fan), or gas mark 4.

In a sauté pan, heat the rapeseed oil on a high heat. Add the rabbit pieces and seal the meat on all sides. In the same hot pan, add the onion, thyme stalks, half the bulb of garlic (crushed lightly), black pepper and Cognac.

Flambé until the flames die down, then add 1 tbsp honey, the cayenne pepper and cornflour. Mix thoroughly.

Turn everything into a baking dish, uncovered, and place in the oven for 50 minutes.

To Make The Sauce
Using the same pan on a high heat, place the lardons in the pan (no oil required) and sauté for approx 5 minutes to colour. Pour off the fat created from the lardons and continue to fry in the dry pan until the lardons are golden brown - this shouldn't take more than about 5 minutes. Add the other half of the garlic bulb, the quartered tomatoes and the remaining 1 tbsp of honey. Simmer for 15 minutes. Add the white wine and continue to simmer, uncovered, for an additional 10 minutes. Finally, add the sliced mushrooms and crème fraîche. Cover the pan and simmer for another 5 minutes. Remove from the heat and sprinkle with torn tarragon and 2 tbsp of extra virgin olive oil.

To Serve
When the rabbit is finished in the oven, pour the sauce over. Serve immediately with a drizzle of lemon juice squeezed over at the last minute.

Boeuf Bourguignon
Beef in Claret Sauce

Serves: **6**
Preparation Time: **20 minutes**
Plus 30 minutes to marinate beef
Cooking Time: **2 hours**

Ingredients

1kg stewing steak
(cut into 2cm cubes)
½ tsp smoked paprika
1 sprig thyme
½ tsp Szechuan peppercorns
2 cloves garlic
(sliced in 2 lengthways)
3 bay leaves
1 tbsp extra virgin rapeseed oil
3 large onions
(peeled and quartered)
2 tsp cornflour
(mixed with 1 tbsp cold water)
700ml good quality claret wine
3 carrots (sliced)
large tin (400g) chopped,
plum tomatoes
½ tsp honey
2 Portobello mushrooms
(peeled and sliced)

Garnish
1 clove garlic (crushed)
2 tbsp extra virgin olive oil
1 small bunch parsley (torn)

Method

Preheat the oven to 180ºC (fan), 200ºC (non-fan),
or gas mark 6.

Marinate the beef in a bowl with the smoked paprika,
thyme, Szechuan peppercorns, garlic bulb and bay leaves
for approx 30 minutes.

Using a hot, deep, non-stick sauté pan with a lid and no
oil or fat, add the meat and fry for 5-10 minutes with the
lid on, turning occasionally. Add a little water, about 50ml
(espresso cup size), and keep on a high heat - this helps
to extract the fat from the meat - continue to braise the
meat for a further 5 minutes. Strain the meat over a bowl
and when the liquid is cold, dispose of it.

Chef's Tip

Leaving the peel on the carrots and just washing increases the amount of vitamin C in your meal. Olive oil must generally be added once all the cooking has been done otherwise all the goodness present in olive oil disappears with heat.

Bourguignon is the term for beef that has been marinated in red wine and cooked in its marinade.

Using the same hot sauté pan, heat the rapeseed oil. Add the meat and the onions. Mix thoroughly with a wooden spatula. Stir in the cornflour mix, then introduce the wine and carrots, making sure that the liquid covers everything in the pan. Bring to the boil, then reduce to a simmer. After approx 15 minutes of simmering, skim the impurities off the top of the liquid, then add the tomatoes and honey and stir. Cover and place into the hot oven for 50-60 minutes.

Reduce the heat of the oven to 140ºC (fan), 160ºC (non-fan), or gas mark 3. Add the mushrooms and cook for a further 50 minutes, or until the meat is nice and tender.

To Finish
Infuse the olive oil with the torn parsley and crushed garlic.

When the meat in the oven is tender, transfer it to the hob, on a low heat, with the lid on. Bring to a slow simmer, then add the oil infusion and immediately switch off the heat. Leave covered until ready to serve.

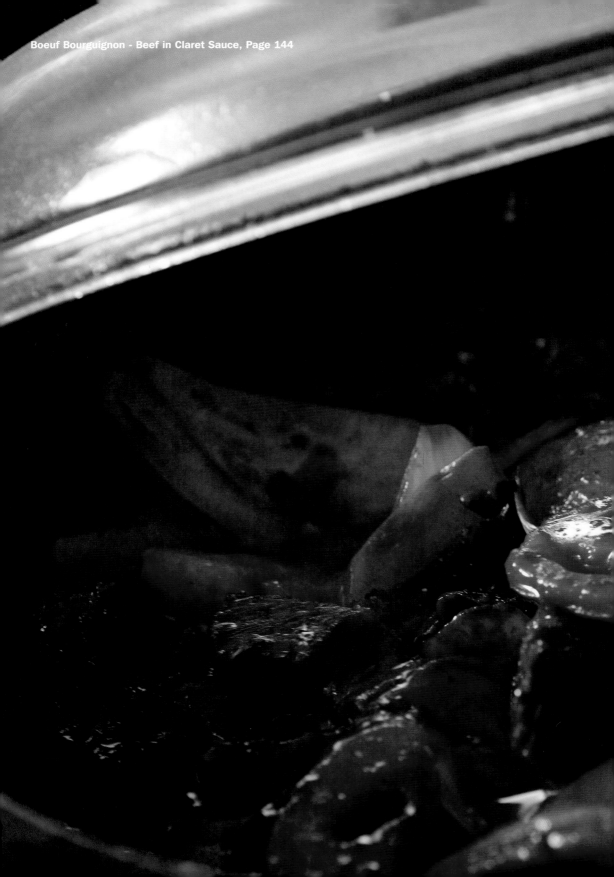

Carbonnade Flamande ou Ch'ti Traditional Beef Carbonnade from the Ch'ti Region of France

This recipe is a close cousin of boeuf bourguignon, but instead of using wine, the meat is cooked in beer which originates from Pas-de-Calais in northern France.

Serves: **6-8**
Preparation Time: **20 minutes**
Soak meat in beer overnight
Cooking Time: **1 hour 45 minutes**

Ingredients

1kg good quality, lean braising steak (cut into 2cm cubes)
extra virgin rapeseed oil (for sautéing)
3 onions (sliced)
3 tbsp brown sugar
2 tbsp balsamic or cider vinegar
10 baby turnips
1ltr blonde beer (eg Leffe, warmed - see tip)
½ tsp juniper berries
1 sprig thyme
2 bay leaves
1 tbsp tomato purée
3 whole chicory/endives (separated and kept in ice cold water until required)
500g mushrooms (halved if small, quartered if large)
fresh bread to serve

Method

Preheat the oven to 160ºC (fan), 180ºC (non-fan), or gas mark 4.

Prepare The Meat The Day Before
Cube the meat and place in a bowl. Pour over the beer and cover with clingfilm. Keep in the fridge overnight. Drain the meat through a sieve, over a bowl. Retain the liquid, which can be warmed separately (see tip).

In a hot sauté pan with a lid, sweat the onions with the sugar and vinegar using the oil. This will change to a dark colour before caramelising. At this point, add the drained meat and cook over a high heat with the lid on. After about 5 minutes, add the turnips and the warmed beer. When the liquid is boiling, skim the impurities. Add the juniper berries, thyme, bay leaves and tomato purée and bring to the boil. Transfer to the hot oven for 1½ hours.

After 1½ hours, if you feel that there is too much liquid, return the pan to the stove and reduce a little of the liquid. Add the chicory leaves and mushrooms (or aubergines - see tip) and return to the oven for a further hour. Serve this wonderful dish with fresh bread straight from the pan.

Chef's Tip

Before adding the beer, heat separately in order to reduce the amount of foam (impurities) that appear on the top. Mushrooms can be substituted with aubergines that have been quartered lengthways and diced into 2cm cubes.

150

Choucroute
Braised Pork Belly Served with Cabbage Stew

Serves: **4-6**
Preparation Time: **20 minutes**
Marinate the cabbage the day before
Cooking Time: **2 hours 30 minutes**

Ingredients

For The Cabbage
1 white cabbage
(halved and finely sliced)
4 onions (finely sliced)
½ celeriac
(peeled and grated - keep the peel)
1½ tsp caraway seeds
1 tsp mustard seeds
8 juniper berries
4 cloves
1 sprig thyme
1 bulb garlic (halved width-ways)
4 bay leaves
75ml white wine vinegar
2 tbsp sugar
extra white wine vinegar or white
wine (if required, to add extra flavour)

For The Pork Belly
600g pork belly
(with the skin on and cut in half)
600g smoked pancetta (chopped)
4 sage leaves
1 small saucisson sec à l'ail
(or any hard salami type sausage - whole)

4 Toulouse sausages
(or any type of herb sausage)
8 Chantenay carrots
(or 4 normal sized carrots)
12 baby new potatoes
1 tbsp extra virgin olive oil

Optional Extras
100ml juice from the meat
1 tbsp mustard
1 tsp parsley (chopped)
2 tbsp extra virgin olive oil

Method

The Day Before
In a large bowl, place the finely sliced cabbage, 2 finely sliced onions, grated celeriac (but not the peel), caraway seeds, mustard seeds, juniper berries, cloves, thyme, half the garlic bulb and bay leaves. Mix thoroughly, then add 75ml of the white wine vinegar, the sugar and mix again. Cover with clingfilm and place in the fridge overnight.

Chef's Tip

During the meat cooking process, after approx 1 hour, the pork belly can be removed and the fat taken off easily and the meat replaced back in the pan to help reduce the fat content of this dish. Or, if you do not like too much fat, pork knuckle can be a substituted for the pork belly.

It has been said that this recipe dates back to the 3rd Century and originates from China. The builders who helped build the Great Wall of China used to eat this dish. Somehow it was exported to the Alsace, where my mother showed me how to make this wonderful meal.

On The Day Of Cooking

Heat a large pan, with a lid. Place the pork belly, pancetta, saucisson and sausages into the pan, cover with water and bring to the boil. Continue to boil for 5 minutes, then turn off the heat. Skim any froth that may have appeared on the top - these are the impurities from the meat. Strain.

Replace the meat into the pan and cover again with fresh cold water. Then add another 2 finely sliced onions, the other half of the garlic bulb and carrots. Make sure the water just about covers everything. Bring to the boil and simmer for 1 hour 15 minutes, with the lid on, skimming the impurities every 15-20 minutes.

After 1 hour 15 minutes, add the potatoes and skin from the celeriac. Continue simmering and skimming for a further 45 minutes.

Before the meat has finished cooking, remove the cabbage mix from the fridge and taste. White wine or extra white wine vinegar may be required for additional flavour. Place all the cabbage into a large pan, with a lid, bring to the boil and then simmer for 25 minutes, covered.

Optional Extra

For added flavour, take approx 100ml of juice from the meat, add 1 tbsp mustard (Dijon or English), 1 tbsp chopped parsley and 2 tbsp extra virgin olive oil and add to the cabbage.

To Serve

Using a large serving bowl, cover the base with the cabbage, then a layer of the meat followed by the potatoes. If using the optional extra sauce, pour gently over the entire dish. If not, just cover with the hot sauce from the pan. Add a drizzle of olive oil at the end to enhance the colours of the dish.

Côtes de Porc Piquantes
Spicy Pork Chops

A rustic dish favoured by hunters and originally made with wild boar.

Serves: **4**
Preparation Time: **10 minutes**
Cooking Time: **30 minutes**

Ingredients

4 lean pork chops
1 tsp coriander seeds
1 tsp mustard seeds
1 sprig thyme
4 sage leaves
½ bulb garlic
(lightly crushed, unpeeled)
5 shallots (sliced)
350ml white wine
2 tbsp sherry vinegar
2 tsp honey
1 tsp harissa paste
3 tbsp crème fraîche
10 cornichon gherkins (chopped)

Chef's Tip

Remove the meat from the fridge 30 minutes before cooking. This will allow it to reach room temperature.

Method

In a very hot sauté pan with a lid and no fat added, add the pork chops and seal. When cooked, remove from the pan and set aside. Cover with clingfilm. Pour the leftover fat into a bowl and dispose of it once cold.

Into the same pan, add the coriander seeds, mustard seeds, thyme, sage, garlic and shallots and stir. Add the white wine, sherry vinegar, honey and harissa. Reduce slowly to the same consistency as thick cream. If the sauce is too runny, and you do not have enough time to reduce to a thick consistency, add a little cornflour mixed with cold water to the sauce - this will help to speed up the thickening process.

To Serve
Reheat the sauce slowly. Add the meat and the crème fraîche, heating slowly. Finally, add the cornichons just before serving.

Mouton Boulangère
Slow Cooked Mutton with Potatoes

This is a favourite dish of mine using a cut of meat rarely used these days.

Serves: **4-6**
Preparation Time: **15 minutes**
Cooking Time: **1 hour 40 minutes**

Ingredients

4-6 mutton chops
2 bay leaves
1 sprig rosemary
½ tsp fennel seeds
½ tsp cumin seeds
4 large onions (sliced)
1 bulb garlic (halved, unpeeled)
1 tsp honey
6 medium sized potatoes
(unpeeled and thinly sliced)
½ celeriac (thinly sliced)
100g Beaufort cheese
(or mature Cheddar)
250ml white wine or Vermouth
400ml hot, strong lamb or vegetable stock
3 tbsp extra virgin rapeseed oil

Chef's Tip

This dish is best prepared the day before, with the final baking process being done on the day of serving. Lamb can obviously be used as a substitute for mutton.

Method

Preheat the oven to 180°C (fan), 200°C (non-fan), gas mark 6.

Using a hot sauté pan with a lid, dry fry the mutton chops for approx 10 minutes each side - keep the lid on to help generate moisture which helps reduce the fat. Place the covered pan into the oven for a further 30 minutes.

In the meantime, prepare the vegetables. Using another sauté pan, heat a little juice from the mutton in the oven. Add the herbs, sliced onions, spices and garlic and cover. Sweat over a low heat until slightly coloured. Add the honey and stir. Add the potatoes and celeriac and sweat for a further 5 minutes. If the vegetables look a little dry, drizzle over a little oil or stock.

After 30 minutes, remove the mutton from the oven.

Using a large gratin dish, start layering the potatoes with the onions and celeriac. Place the cheese in the middle of the dish. Position a layer of mutton chops around the cheese and drizzle a small amount of juice from the meat pan over the chops. Finish with a final layer of potatoes around the cheese.

Discard the fat left in the pan from the chops, then put the pan back on the heat. Add the stock and wine (or Vermouth) and bring to the boil. Skim any residue that may now appear from the surface. Pour over the potatoes until all are covered.

Cover the gratin dish with foil and place into the oven for 30 minutes at 180°C (fan), then for 10 minutes at a slightly lower temperature of 160°C (fan), 180° (non-fan), or gas mark 4. After 10 minutes, lift the foil carefully from the gratin dish and check that there is a thick sauce formed over the potatoes and meat. If this hasn't happened, place back in the oven, uncovered, for a further 10 minutes.

Serve from the pan in the centre of your table.

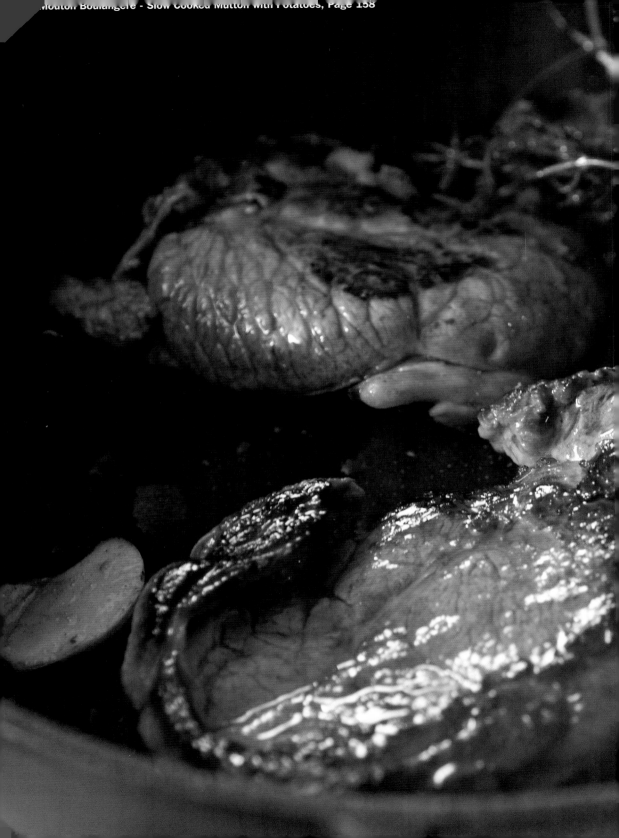

Navarin ou Ragôut D'Agneaux
Navarin of Lamb

Some say this dish is named after The Battle of Navarino 1827 and others say it comes from the word navet, meaning turnip. I'm not sure which one to believe, but naming it after a battle sounds more romantic!

Serves: **6**
Preparation Time: **20 minutes**
Cooking Time: **80 minutes**

Ingredients

1kg lamb neck fillet (in 1 piece)
2 tbsp extra virgin olive oil
1 onion (quartered)
2 shallots (quartered lengthways)
crushed black pepper
1 bay leaf
1 sprig rosemary
1 sprig thyme
½ tsp coriander seeds
½ tsp cayenne pepper
500ml hot vegetable stock
70g tomato purée
400g chopped, tinned plum tomatoes
1 bulb garlic (halved widthways, unpeeled)
10 baby new potatoes
10 baby turnips (halved lengthways)
3 large carrots (halved lengthways, unpeeled)
2 tsp brown sugar
50g plain flour
1 bunch fresh parsley (chopped)

Method

Heat a large sauté pan, with a lid. Add the meat, with no oil, browning on all sides whilst covered with the lid. Remove the meat and pour off the fat generated, disposing of it when cool.

Using the same pan on a high heat, sauté the onions and shallots until soft. Add the black pepper, bay leaf, thyme, rosemary, coriander seeds, cayenne pepper and stock. Mix completely, then stir in the tomato purée, chopped tomatoes and garlic bulb. Cover and bring to the boil. Reduce the heat to a simmer for 10 minutes.

After 10 minutes, add the potatoes, turnips, sugar and carrots. Add the flour and return the meat to the pan. Bring back to the boil and then simmer, covered, for 1 hour or until the meat and vegetables are tender.

To Serve
Check the seasoning and serve with chopped parsley sprinkled over the dish.

Chef's Tip

To thicken the sauce, leave the lid off the pan for the last 10 minutes of cooking, but be careful not to reduce too much and leave no sauce!

Parmentier Boudin Noir
Potatoes Sautéed with Black Pudding

Serves: **4**
Preparation Time: **25 minutes**
Cooking Time: **70 minutes**

Ingredients

400g potatoes (unpeeled)
300g celeriac (unpeeled)
10g unsalted butter
3 Granny Smith apples
(quartered, not peeled or cored)
1 lemon (juice of)
600g soft black pudding
(skin removed and cut into cubes)
1 onion (sliced)
1 sprig thyme
1 tbsp fresh sage leaves
½ tsp mild curry powder
1 tsp honey
1 tsp cumin seeds
8 slices bread
2 tbsp extra virgin rapeseed oil
2 tbsp crème fraîche or 100ml
stock (optional for mashing)

Chef's Tip

When preparing the black pudding, 1 tbsp of vinegar over the meat will give it an extra kick of flavour.

This gratin dish was named after a chemist called Antoine Parmentier who believed it was a dish to fight famine during Louis XVI's reign.

Method

Preheat the oven to 200°C (fan), 220°C (non-fan), gas mark 7.

For The Potatoes And Celeriac
Bring a deep pan of water to the boil. Add the unpeeled whole potatoes and celeriac and simmer for 35 minutes. Drain and place on a baking tray. Transfer to the oven for approx 10 minutes to remove most of the moisture.

To Make The Mashed Apple
Place the quartered apples into a sauté pan, with lid. Add the juice from the lemon, the sage and approx 100ml of hot water. Bring to the boil for 5 minutes and then set away from the heat and allow to rest (covered) for 15 minutes. Remove the excess liquid from the apple and mash.

For The Black Pudding Mix
In a hot sauté pan, heat the rapeseed oil. Add the onion, cumin seeds, thyme, sage, curry powder, honey and cubed black pudding. Stir thoroughly and cover. Sauté for 10 minutes.

To Prepare For Baking
Remove the potatoes and celeriac from the oven and replace with the bread, on a baking sheet, for 10 minutes. After 10 minutes, take the bread out and blend into course breadcrumbs. Keep to one side.

Once the potatoes and celeriac are cool enough, squeeze the flesh into a mixing bowl, making sure that the skin is kept separate and discarded. Mash with a potato masher - if the mash is appearing a little dry, add either 2 tablespoons of crème fraîche or 100ml stock to make it smooth.

Reduce the temperature of the oven to 180°C (fan), 200°C (non-fan), or gas mark 6.

In a deep-sided oven dish, make a layer of mashed apple, then a layer of the black pudding mixture, a layer of potato and celeriac mixture and a sprinkle of breadcrumbs.

To Serve
Place in the oven for 25 minutes and serve.

Steak au Poivre
Steak in Pepper Sauce

A traditional French classic dish. Good quality steak, usually Filet Mignon, covered in a peppercorn sauce.

Serves: **4**
Preparation Time: **30 minutes**
Cooking Time: **15 minutes**

Ingredients

4 fillet steaks
4 tbsp extra virgin rapeseed oil
½ tsp chilli powder (optional)
½ bulb garlic (unpeeled)

For The Sauce
10ml Cognac (optional)
200ml double cream, or half-fat crème fraîche
1 tbsp mixed peppercorns
(pounded a little in a pestle and mortar)
1 tbsp chopped parsley

Chef's Tip

Different cuts of steak require different amounts of oil for frying, due to their fat content. No fat is required for rib-eye, rump and sirloin cuts as they already have plenty of fat content.

The infused oil can be brushed on after frying to add flavour.

Method

To begin, remove the steaks from the fridge for 30 minutes to get them to room temperature.

Infuse the oil with the chilli powder.

Using a large plate, cover the meat with the oil on both sides and set aside until ready to cook.

Use a large, very hot, sauté pan. Place the steaks into the pan with the half bulb of garlic and sauté for approx 4 minutes on each side. This will probably give you a medium cooked steak, depending obviously on thickness. Remove from the pan and rest in a warm place.

For The Sauce
Using the same pan, add the Cognac and flambé. Allow to reduce for 1 minute. Remove from the heat and when cooled, add the cream, peppercorns and parsley. Let it infuse a little.

When ready to serve, and the meat has rested for about 5 minutes, return to the pan and heat gently in the peppercorn sauce. Serve immediately.

Great served with chunky French fries.

Veau aux Abricots Secs
Veal with Dried Apricots

A hearty dish, ideal for a cold winter's night. Since this recipe originates from Morocco, it is usually made in a traditional tagine.

Serves: **4**
Preparation Time: **10 minutes**
Cooking Time: **35 minutes**

Ingredients

750g veal escalope
(sliced into 4 slices)
1 large onion (sliced)
2 tbsp sherry vinegar
1 tbsp honey
1 cinnamon stick
½ tsp cumin seeds
16 dried apricots
(soaked in hot water for 15 minutes,
then strained and cut in half)
100g raisins (soaked in hot water for
15 minutes, then strained)
crushed black pepper (to taste)

plain steamed rice (to serve)

Chef's Tip

To add another dimension to the sauce, pour half a glass (40ml) of Kirsch into the sauce before reducing - this is optional.

Method

Heat a good quality, non-stick pan, with a tight fitting lid, to a high heat, add the veal and cover immediately. Seal (no oil required) for 3 minutes on each side. Remove the veal and keep in a warm place. Dispose of the fat.

Using the same pan, add the sliced onions and sauté with the lid on. Add the vinegar, spices and enough water to just about cover the onions (this will vary with the size of the pan used). Reintroduce the meat and throw in the fruits and sauté with the lid on for approx 30 minutes until the sauce has reduced and has thickened.

To Serve
Serve with plain steamed rice. Place the veal on top of the rice and pour the thick, reduced sauce over the veal before serving.

Couscous de mon Voisin
Couscous Made My Neighbour's Way!

Serves: **4-6**
Preparation Time: **30 minutes**
Cooking Time: **90 minutes**

Ingredients

1kg neck of lamb fillet (large dice)
2 chicken legs
(cut through the joint to create 4 pieces)
2 onions (quartered)
4 baby carrots (whole)
2 baby turnips (halved lengthways)
½ celeriac (large dice)
50g fresh ginger
(peeled and thinly sliced)
1 tsp coriander seeds
½ tsp turmeric powder
1 tsp cumin seeds
½ bulb garlic
400g tin chopped tomatoes
1 courgette
(chopped into large pieces)
1 aubergine
(chopped into large pieces)
400g tin chickpeas
2 tbsp tomato purée
500ml hot lamb/vegetable stock
1 sweet potato (sliced into thirds)
1 bulb fennel (quartered and diced)
100g raisins
1-2 tbsp harissa paste

Couscous
450g couscous
4 tbsp extra virgin olive oil
½ tsp mild curry powder
½ tsp turmeric
400ml hot lamb/vegetable stock

Garnish
fresh green herbs

Chef's Tip

Just boiling something is classed as
interfering. Simmering is clarification.
Boiling + Simmering = Cooking!

Basically, as this title says, I was taught this recipe by my family's
neighbour where we used to spend time as a child.

Method

In a very hot, deep pan with a lid,
seal the lamb. Add the chicken
pieces and seal altogether. Add the
onions, carrots, turnips, celeriac and
ginger. Place the lid onto the pan
and shake the ingredients. Next,
add the coriander seeds, turmeric,
cumin seeds, the half garlic bulb
and the tinned tomatoes. Stir, then
add the chickpeas and the tomato
purée and stir again. Add the stock
to cover everything in the pan
(approx 500ml). Cover with the lid.
Bring to the boil and reduce to a
simmer for 30 minutes.

After 30 minutes of cooking, add the
rest of the vegetables and bring back
to a simmer (not boiling at all!).
Cover and leave to simmer for 30
minutes. Taste the sauce and adjust
the seasoning. At this point, add the
harissa and dried raisins and continue
to simmer for a further 30 minutes.

To Prepare The Couscous
Using a stainless steel or large glass bowl, mix the
couscous and the olive oil with your hands. Add the curry
powder and turmeric, then approx 400ml of stock. Stir
using a fork and cover with clingfilm. After 10 minutes or
so, the couscous can be stirred lightly with the fork and
served immediately.

To Serve
Place the couscous on a large serving plate or bowl.
Spoon the meat and vegetables into the middle of the
dish and decorate with green herbs. Serve immediately.

Canard à l'Orange
Duck in Orange Sauce

A very popular dish both in France and around Europe. Duck in orange sauce has been sold all over Paris since 1945.

Serves: **4**
Preparation Time: **15 minutes**
Cooking Time: **1 hour 40 minutes**

Ingredients

1 whole duck
3 large sweet potatoes
(washed, unpeeled, cut into 2cm slices)
½ garlic bulb
(unpeeled, halved widthways)
2 cardamom pods
4 shallots (sliced)
2 oranges (juice of)
1 grapefruit (juice of)
1 tsp fennel seeds
2 tbsp honey
½ vanilla pod (halved lengthways)

Chef's Tip

If you prefer your potatoes to be nice and dry, place them on a baking tray in the oven for 15 minutes at a high heat before plating them with the duck.

Method

Preheat the oven to 200ºC (fan), 220ºC (non-fan), or gas mark 7.

In a roasting pan, layer the sliced sweet potatoes and garlic. Place the duck on top of the potatoes - this acts similar to a trivet on the bottom of the pan. Roast for 45 minutes on the high heat.

Remove the duck from the oven and reduce the temperature to 160ºC (fan), 180ºC (non-fan), or gas mark 4.

Carefully pour the juices from the bottom of the pan into a bowl and dispose of this when cold.

Place the duck back into the oven at the reduced temperature for 30-45 minutes, depending on size.

When ready, remove the duck from the oven. Place the duck and potatoes onto a dish and cover with clingfilm to keep warm. Put the roasting pan on the hob and heat the juices. Add the cardamom pods and shallots and sweat until the shallots are soft. Then add the vanilla, honey, orange juice, fennel seeds and grapefruit juice and reduce, on a high heat, for approx 10 minutes to produce a thick sauce.

To Serve
Place the duck on a large serving plate and decorate with the sweet potatoes and garlic. Using a large serving spoon, drizzle the now thick sauce over the duck and serve immediately.

Coq aux Vin avec Chocolat - Chicken in Red
Wine & Chocolate, Page 182

Chef's Tip

If you can, use a rooster, it will improve the flavours and texture of the dish. It will probably need a little longer in the oven, depending on size.

This dish can be traced back as far as the conquest of Gaul by Julius Caesar, where a tribal leader of the Arverne tribe taunted the Romans by sending Caesar a rooster, which was a symbol of Gaul bravery. Caesar, in return, invited him to eat the rooster which he'd had cooked in red wine.

Method

Preheat the oven to 180°C (fan), 200°C (non-fan), or gas mark 6.

Seal the chicken pieces in a very hot, large non-stick sauté pan, with a lid, and brown them all over. Add approx 100ml water to help to speed up this process. Remove the chicken and set aside on a plate. Pour away the excess fat and juices from the pan.

In the same pan, on a moderate heat, add the onions, shallots and garlic then cover. Cook slowly for a couple of minutes, then introduce the cumin seeds, thyme, bay, rosemary and smoked paprika. Continue to sauté slowly. After approx 10-15 minutes the onions should be soft.

At this point, add the cocoa powder and honey, stirring continuously - otherwise it will burn. Return the chicken to the pan and stir in the cornflour mixed with water. Combine thoroughly. Add the wine, enough to cover everything in the pan. Then, with the lid on, bring to the boil and simmer. Once simmering, skim any impurities that have collected on the top of the sauce using a large spoon or ladle. Add the vanilla pod and taste. Adjust the seasoning. Cover and place the pan into the preheated oven for 50 minutes with the lid on, followed by 15 minutes without the lid on.

Just before serving, infuse the herbs with the olive oil and drizzle over the dish to lift the colours.

Serve with plain boiled white basmati rice.

Poule au Pot
Chicken in a Pot

Henry IV announced that no peasant will
go without a chicken in his pot!

Serves: **4**
Preparation Time: **20 minutes**
Cooking Time: **80 minutes**

Ingredients

1 whole chicken
(cut into 4 pieces, legs and breast)
4 baby leeks (quartered lengthways)
1 onion (quartered)
4 shallots (quartered lengthways)
1 fennel (quartered lengthways)
½ celeriac (quartered)
4 baby turnips (quartered)
6 baby carrots (halved)
1 sprig thyme
2 bay leaves
1 garlic bulb (halved)
1 sprig rosemary
1 tsp black peppercorns
1½ tbsp plain flour
1½ tsp white sugar

To Serve
2 tbsp extra virgin olive oil mixed
with 1 tbsp chopped basil

Method

Using a hot, deep, large pan with a lid, add the leeks,
onions, shallots, celeriac, turnips, carrots, thyme, fennel,
garlic, bay leaves, rosemary and peppercorns. Cover and
shake the pan, but do not allow the vegetables to colour.
Add a little water and cover, shaking occasionally to
extract the flavours and humidity created by this process.
Continue for 2 minutes, then cover the vegetables with
water and simmer for 20 minutes, covered.

Add the chicken pieces, making sure there is enough
liquid to cover all the pieces. Simmer for 40 minutes.

After 40 minutes, remove approx 100ml of the stock
and mix with the flour, using a wooden spatula, to create
a roux (paste).

Turn the heat down on the stew and start adding the
roux, 1 tablespoon at a time. Mix in thoroughly each time
- this will thicken the sauce. Taste, and add a little sugar
if required.

To Serve
Remove all the vegetables and place on a large serving
platter or bowl. Place the chicken pieces on top and cover
with the thick sauce. Drizzle with basil infused olive oil
before serving.

Chef's Tip

Once everyone has eaten the chicken, you may have
stock left over in the pot. This can be frozen and used
as a marvellous chicken stock in other recipes.

187

Poulet Provençale à la Moutarde
Chicken Provençale with Mustard

This recipe originates from the south west of France where the rolling hills of Provence meet the blue waters of the Mediterranean.

Serves: **4**
Preparation Time: **30 minutes**
Cooking Time: **40 minutes**

Ingredients

4 chicken legs
(cut through the joint to separate drumsticks and thighs)
2 tbsp extra virgin olive oil
1 tbsp eau de vie (or Cognac)
3 shallots (sliced)
1 yellow pepper (diced)
1 whole fennel (diced)
1 sprig rosemary
crushed black pepper (to taste)
½ garlic bulb
1 courgette (diced)
1 sprig fresh basil
3 plum tomatoes (diced)
350ml dry white wine
2 tsp cornflour
(mixed with 2 tsp cold water)
1 tbsp mixed olives
2 tbsp wholegrain mustard

pasta or brown basmati rice
(to serve)

Method

Preheat the oven to 160ºC (fan), 180ºC (non-fan), or gas mark 4.

To Seal The Chicken
In a deep pan with a lid, heat a little oil and sauté the chicken legs to seal and colour them. Set aside the chicken and pour off the excess fat from the pan. Return to the heat.

For The Sauce
Pour the eau de vie into the pan, heat for 30 seconds, then ignite to flambé. Add the shallots, yellow pepper, fennel, rosemary, black pepper and garlic, then sauté for 10 minutes. At the last minute, add the courgettes with the torn basil and cover with a lid.

To Cook The Chicken And Serve
Return the chicken to the pan, add the tomatoes, white wine and cornflour. Cover and put into the oven for 20 minutes or more (depending on the size of the chicken). Just before serving, place back on the hob and introduce the olives. Stir in the mustard, but do not let it boil. Serve.

Perfect with pasta or boiled brown basmati rice.

Chef's Tip

The cooking times will need to be adjusted according to the size of the chicken legs used for this recipe.

Cannelloni de Risotto aux Légumes

Risotto & Vegetables Wrapped in Cabbage Cannelloni

Serves: **4**
Preparation Time: **15 minutes**
Cooking Time: **40 minutes**

Ingredients

1 aubergine
(roughly cut into uneven pieces)
1 courgette
(roughly cut into uneven pieces)
1 plum tomato
(roughly cut into uneven pieces)
1 onion (roughly cut into uneven pieces)
1 yellow pepper
(roughly cut into uneven pieces)
5 tbsp extra virgin rapeseed oil
1 tsp smoked paprika
1 tsp sugar
10 olives
200g Arborio rice
1 ltr strong, hot vegetable stock
2 tbsp fresh parsley and basil
(chopped)
50g ricotta or mascarpone cheese
100g Gruyère/Comté/strong
Cheddar cheese (grated)
6 Savoy cabbage leaves

Chef's Tip

Before placing the parcels into the oven, mix the remaining grated cheese into the stock with one crushed garlic clove and a drizzle of extra virgin olive oil. Pour this over the parcels before baking. This will give a richer taste to the dish.

The mixture can be put into the cabbage leaves the day before using and then baked when required. Remove from the fridge 30 minutes before baking.

This dish has been influenced by the migration of ideas from our neighbours in Italy.

Method

To Prepare The Vegetables
Heat the rapeseed oil in a hot sauté pan. Using a small knife, cut the vegetables in a non-uniform manner directly into a pan. If you are worried about this, cut on a cutting board into large dice approx 2cm in size. This prevents the vegetables from cooking too quickly and becoming mushy in the rice.

For The Risotto
Stir thoroughly and cover the roughly cut vegetables and onions, (with the exception of the cabbage leaves), paprika and sugar. Sauté for approx 5 minutes. Add the olives and the rice then stir.

Make sure your stock is really hot, then start adding one ladle at a time, stirring between ladles. Once you have added approx ½ litre of stock, keep stirring until the liquid evaporates. Taste to see if the rice is cooked. If not, add some more stock, a ladle at a time, and keep checking by tasting.

Once the rice is cooked and the liquid has all evaporated, add the chopped green herbs. Stir, then mix in the ricotta and half of the grated hard cheese.

To Cook The Cabbage Leaves
Place your cabbage leaves into the remaining hot stock for 3 minutes, then remove.

To Serve
Preheat the oven to 160ºC (fan), 180ºC (non-fan), or gas mark 4.

Place a cabbage leaf onto a flat surface, spoon a little of the risotto into the middle of the leaf and roll the leaf up to form cannelloni shaped parcels. Continue until all the leaves are filled and rolled. Pour a little stock into an ovenproof (gratin) dish, then arrange the parcels in the dish.

Cover the cabbage parcels with the remaining grated cheese. Bake for 20 minutes and serve. See tip for an alternative finishing option.

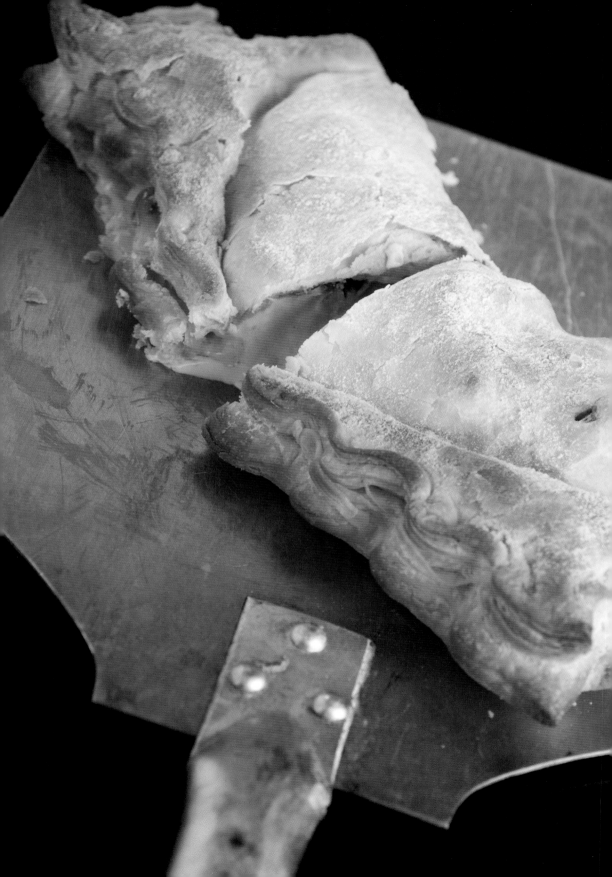

Chausson Vichyssoise
Potato & Celeriac
Puff Pastry Parcels

Created in the Ritz-Carlton in 1917, this dish has appeared in many forms ever since.

Serves: **4**
Preparation Time: **20 minutes**
Cooking Time: **40 minutes**

Ingredients

300g potatoes (peeled and cubed)
200g celeriac (peeled and cubed)
300g onions (sliced)
1 tbsp pumpkin seeds
(lightly toasted in a dry pan)
150ml crème fraîche
1 tbsp tarragon (freshly chopped)
grated nutmeg (pinch of)
100g Reblochon or Époisses cheese (cubed)
crushed black pepper (to taste)
1 tbsp melted butter
100g puff pastry (rolled very thin to approx the size of an A4 sheet of paper)

Chef's Tip

Make sure the potatoes and celeriac are very dry, otherwise the pastry may become soggy when cooking.

Method

Preheat an oven to 180°C (fan), 200°C (non-fan), or gas mark 6.

For The Potatoes
In a deep pan, heat enough water to cover all the ingredients. Once it reaches boiling point, add the potatoes. After 5 minutes, add the celeriac and simmer for 15 minutes - not too long that they go to mash. Drain thoroughly for about 20 minutes in a colander to make sure all the water has evaporated (see chef's tip).

In a separate, hot sauté pan with a lid, add the onions. Cover and let them sweat for a short while. Then, add the pumpkin seeds, nutmeg, pepper and tarragon then stir. Introduce the potatoes and celeriac back into the pan, reduce the heat, add the crème fraîche and simmer for 5 minutes. Remove from the heat and place in the fridge.

To Assemble
On a floured surface, lay out the pastry. Place the cold mixture in the middle of the pastry. Brush the edges with a little melted butter and close up the parcel. Place on a baking tray and bake for between 15-20 minutes.

Serve with a salad or as an accompaniment to fish or meat.

Gnocchi de Patates Douces
Sweet Potato Gnocchi

This dish has evolved from the Italian influences which have migrated into France over the years, with a slight influence from North Africa with the sweet potato twist.

Serves: **4**
Preparation Time: **15 minutes**
Cooking Time: **20 minutes**

Ingredients

800g sweet potatoes
(whole and unpeeled)
2 eggs (beaten)
1 tbsp crème fraîche
320g plain flour
¼ tsp nutmeg (grated)
1 sprig thyme
120g Parmesan cheese
1 tbsp extra virgin rapeseed oil
2 cloves garlic (crushed)

Method

Preheat the oven to 160ºC (fan), 180ºC (non-fan), or gas mark 4.

Cut the sweet potatoes lengthways in half and place on a baking tray. Place in the oven and bake for approx 30 minutes. After 15 minutes, turn the potatoes over. When soft, remove from the oven. When cold, carefully remove the skin and pass all the sweet potato through a mouli or fine sieve.

Add the beaten eggs and crème fraîche to the warm mash, then stir in the flour, nutmeg and thyme. Mix thoroughly until you have a nice soft dough. Add the Parmesan cheese and mix until you have a thick texture - similar to cement!

Using a little flour on the work surface, roll narrow cylinders of dough and cut into 2cm lengths. Using a fork, press one side down to leave an imprint on the cylinder.

To Serve

Steam the dough cylinders for 3 minutes, or boil in water until they float to the top of the pan. Drain the gnocchi.

In a sauté pan, heat the oil, add the garlic and sauté the gnocchi for 2 minutes then serve.

Chef's Tip

Serve with a spoonful of homemade, infused tomato sauce (see recipe page 110).

Little Jean's Pizza

I used to watch my mother cooking when I was a child. I try to show my children as much action in the kitchen as possible so they grow up loving food as much as I do.

Serves: **4 kids**
Preparation Time: **20 minutes**
Cooking Time: **8 minutes**

Ingredients

Dough
300g strong bread flour
10g fresh yeast
3g sugar
1 tbsp olive oil
150-200ml warm water

Tomato Sauce
100g tomatoes (chopped)
fresh basil (handful of)
1 clove garlic (crushed)

Topping
4 Mini Babybel cheeses (sliced)
(Leerdammer is a great alternative.
We need to use more as I like to eat it
whilst daddy isn't looking!)
handful cherry tomatoes (halved)

To Finish
handful fresh basil leaves (optional)
75g peas (should have been broccoli
but daddy did not buy any!)

Method

Bake in a pizza oven, or preheat an oven to 220ºC (fan), 240ºC (non-fan), or gas mark 9.

To Make The Dough
Mix the yeast and sugar in the water.

Put the flour into a large bowl and make a well. Pour in the yeast mixture and the olive oil. Bring together with a wooden spoon (I like to use my hand) until you have a soft, fairly wet dough. Turn out onto a lightly floured surface and knead for 5 minutes until smooth (this is hard work, get a grown-up to help you do it!). Cover with a tea towel and set aside. You can leave the dough to rise if you like, but it's not essential for a thin crust.

To Make The Sauce
Mix the tomato, basil and crushed garlic together, then season to taste. Leave to stand at room temperature while you get on with shaping the base.

To Finish
If you choose to let the dough rise, give it a quick knead, then split into two balls. On a floured surface, roll out the dough into large rounds, about 25cm across, using a rolling pin. The dough needs to be very thin as it will get bigger in the oven.

I like to roll out the dough, but my daddy moans at the mess I make. Flour everywhere!

Top with the tomato sauce, add the broccoli (my very favourite vegetable), or peas and the cherry tomatoes. Finally, sprinkle the cheese over everything.

Bake for 8-10 minutes until the base is crispy - I do not like the hot oven so I get mummy or daddy to help with this.

Yummy!

Patates Douces Roties avec Pignons de Pin
Roasted Sweet Potatoes with Cocoa & Pine Kernels

Sweet potatoes are a staple food in my household and are high in natural sugars. My kids love them as an alternative to normal potatoes. Try them, and I'm sure if you have kids, they will love them too!

Serves: **4**
Preparation Time: **15 minutes**
Cooking Time: **25 minutes**

Ingredients

1kg sweet potatoes
(peeled and sliced into 1cm slices)
150g pine kernels
4 tsp extra virgin rapeseed oil
1 tsp fresh ginger (grated)
½ vanilla pod (halved lengthways)
3 sage leaves
1 tsp honey
1 tsp thyme (leaves only)
½ bulb garlic
½ tsp cocoa powder

Method

Preheat the oven to 180ºC (fan), 200ºC (non-fan), or gas mark 6.

Scatter the pine kernels on the baking tray and bake for 5 minutes.

In a large sauté pan, gently warm the oil and add the grated ginger. Stir, then add the vanilla pod, sage, thyme, garlic and honey. Stir very quickly, then add the cocoa powder whilst stirring. Mix in the uncooked, peeled and sliced sweet potatoes and the roasted pine kernels. Place the pan into the oven and bake for 15 minutes, then reduce the heat to 160ºC (fan), 180ºC (non-fan), or gas mark 5 for a further 5 minutes, or longer if required. Check that the sweet potatoes are cooked and serve.

Chef's Tip

As the sweet potatoes are quite sweet and contain a considerable amount of natural sugars, they will colour themselves so the honey can be left out if you find that the potatoes at that particular time of year are sweeter.

For an additional 'kick' add the juice of half a lemon and throw in some fresh rocket leaves just before serving.

Soufflé aux Épinards
Spinach Soufflé

Soufflés have always been popular in France and this vegetarian version is always a favourite in my home.

Serves: **4**
Preparation Time: **40 minutes**
Cooking Time: **30 minutes**

Ingredients

500g fresh spinach leaves
(washed 30 minutes before required and
left to drain in a colander)
1 garlic clove (crushed)
¼ tsp nutmeg (grated)
¼ tsp crushed black pepper
2 tsp extra virgin rapeseed oil
3 tbsp plain flour
1 sprig fresh basil
1 sprig fresh tarragon
4 egg whites
salt (pinch of)
½ tsp sugar
150g soft goat's cheese or
Camembert-type cheese
(crumbled into very small pieces,
or grated, if possible, after chilling)

4 chilled ramekins

Chef's Tip

In addition to the cheese coating, crushed toasted pine kernels can be lined on the sides and base of the ramekin dishes.

Why not try one of my tasty side dishes to complement this dish!

Method

Preheat the oven to 180°C (fan), 200°C (non-fan), or gas mark 6.

Place the 4 ramekin dishes into the freezer.

Place the spinach into a large pan, on a medium heat with the garlic, nutmeg and black pepper. Allow to wilt, then remove from the heat. Drain using a colander, over a bowl, and retain the liquid. You should get approx 250ml of liquid. Once the spinach has drained, remove and chop roughly. Return to the colander to drain once again.

In the same pan, heat the rapeseed oil and, using only a wooden spoon, mix in the flour to create a roux. Add 200ml of the spinach liquid to the roux and stir thoroughly to create a mornay sauce. Bring to the boil and continue to stir. Add the chopped spinach, roughly torn basil and tarragon and mix into the sauce. Remove from the heat and allow to cool.

Whisk the egg whites, with a pinch of salt, in a mixing bowl, until the whisk leaves marks in the meringue. Add the sugar and continue to whisk for a short while until soft peaks form.

When the spinach mixture is cold, add one third of the whisked egg whites. Stir in thoroughly, then gently fold in the remaining meringue mixture.

Remove the ramekins from the freezer. Using your fingers, coat the base and sides of the ramekins with oil. Then, put some crumbled cheese into each ramekin coating the base and sides evenly.

Pour in the spinach mixture and tap on the work surface to ensure there are no air pockets. Place on a baking tray and bake for 30 minutes. Serve immediately - the soufflés cannot be left too long after they are cooked before eating.

"A little squeeze of half a lemon and a pinch of chilli powder can be added to the caramel to give a totally different taste."

es Desserts

Desserts

Beignets aux Pommes
Apple Fritters

Beignets have been around since the 13th Century. This is a version that I think tastes particularly good.

Serves: **4**
Preparation Time: **35 minutes**
Cooking Time: **40 minutes**

Ingredients

4 Granny Smith apples
(cored and peeled just before using)
½ tsp mild curry powder
250g plain flour
2 whole eggs
3 egg yolks
150ml extra virgin rapeseed oil
300ml beer
(dark French beer if possible, or stout)
1 tsp honey
1 tsp sesame seeds
3 egg whites
rapeseed oil (for deepfrying)
icing sugar (to dust)

Chef's Tip

A good quality, extra virgin rapeseed oil contains less than 6g/100ml of saturated fat. As long as the oil is very hot when used and the food well drained, the fat content in this dish can be moderated.

Method

Preheat the oven to 180°C (fan), 200°C (non-fan), or gas mark 6.

Half the apples lengthways. Place on a non-stick baking tray, or a sheet of silicon on a baking tray, and bake for 15 minutes. Remove from the oven and cover with the curry powder. Place back into the oven for 10 minutes. The juices created around the apples will help the curry powder to be absorbed into the fruit. Remove from the oven and place to one side.

Thoroughly mix the flour, the 2 whole eggs, the 3 egg yolks (not the whites), the oil, beer, honey and sesame seeds in a mixing bowl. Place in a freezer for 45-60 minutes just before using, or if possible, overnight in a fridge.

When ready to serve, whisk the egg whites in a bowl until soft peaks form. Fold into the cold batter from the fridge or freezer.

Preheat the oil to approx 170°C.

Take a piece of apple and place it into the batter, covering it completely. Deepfry in the hot oil for 5 minutes, or until the apple starts to float. Drain on kitchen paper and continue with the other pieces of apple.

Dust with icing sugar and serve.

209

Clafoutis
Clafoutis with Strawberries

Originating from the Limousin region, this is now a popular dish all over France.

Serves: **4**
Preparation Time: **15 minutes**
Cooking Time: **60 minutes**

Ingredients

4 eggs (whisked)
150g sugar
1 vanilla pod
(halved lengthways, seeds scraped out)
100g plain flour
2 tsp baking powder
30g unsalted butter (very soft)
180ml full-fat milk (warmed)
5ml Kirsch (optional)
700g large strawberries (washed,
stalks left on and halved lengthways)
icing sugar (to dust)

Chef's Tip

Other fruits can be used when in season including raspberries, cherries, plums, or apricots.

Method

Preheat the oven to 160°C (fan), 180°C (non-fan), gas mark 4.

Whisk the eggs in a large bowl. Add the sugar and keep whisking, using a hand whisk. Add the seeds of the vanilla pod and continue whisking. Add the plain flour and baking powder and whisk until frothy. Whisk in the butter and introduce the warmed milk, whisking continuously. Add the Kirsch (if using).

Spread the halved strawberries over the base of a gratin or baking dish. Place in the oven for 15 minutes without anything on them, to increase the intensity of their flavour. Do not let them disintegrate. Then, pour the 'custard' mixture over the strawberries until they are covered. Place the dish carefully into the hot oven and bake for approx 35-40 minutes until the top has browned and a knife or skewer comes out clean.

Remove from the oven and sprinkle with sieved icing sugar before serving.

Crème Brûlée
Baked Custard

A version of this recipe can be proven to date back to 17th Century chef of the French court, François Massialot's cookbook from 1691.

Serves: **4**
Preparation Time: **20 minutes**
Cooking Time: **50 minutes**

Ingredients

400ml single cream
4 egg yolks
60g sugar
½ vanilla pod (seeds only)
caramel crunch powder
(see recipe page 274)

4 shallow ramekins

Chef's Tip

Some people recommend that you sprinkle the top of the brûlée with sugar and use a blow torch to caramelise the top to get that crisp sugar topping. This is not necessary, by using my caramel crunch recipe (see page 274) you get the same effect in less time which prevents re-cooking the brûlée underneath.

Method

Preheat the oven to 140°C (fan), 160°C (non-fan), or gas mark 3.

Heat the cream gently in a pan, but do not let it boil. Once warmed, remove from the heat.

In a mixing bowl, beat the egg yolks and add the sugar. Mix thoroughly. Once mixed completely, add a little of the warmed cream and stir into the mixture. Gradually add all of the warmed cream and mix thoroughly, then add the vanilla seeds and stir again.

Place the mixture into 4 shallow ramekin dishes (normally terracotta) and sit in a deep tray filled with water to half way up the ramekin dishes (bain marie) and bake in the oven for approx 50 minutes. When the brûlées have set to the point that they still move when shaking the pan (ie wobble), it's time to take them out of the oven. Sprinkle with coarsely crushed caramel powder and melt with a blow torch. Leave to set then serve.

Douillon de Poire Romarin
Pears in Puff Pastry & Rosemary Sauce

This is my creation combining my love of good fruit and my baking heritage and reminds me of my childhood with my brother Anthony. I just love this dessert.

Serves: **4**
Preparation Time: **35 minutes**
Plus ½ day marinating in syrup
Cooking Time: **20 minutes**

Ingredients

4 large pears (cored and peeled, whole with stalks on)
350ml water
300g sugar
100g fresh rosemary (dried for 10 minutes in an oven at 150ºC (fan), 170ºC (non-fan), or gas mark 3)
3 cloves
100g crème pâtissière (see page 268)
1 tsp rum or Cognac (optional)
4 x 100g prepared puff pastry (shop bought works fine)
1 tbsp pistachios (chopped)
seasonal berries (to decorate)

Chef's Tip

Instead of piping the crème pâtissière directly into the pears, you can pipe cylinders on a plate and freeze them before stuffing the pears. Alternatively, you can place quince, Kirsch or raspberry jam inside the pears instead of the crème pâtissière.

Method

Boil 150ml water in a saucepan and add the sugar. Continue to boil until a golden caramel has been created. Add the warm rosemary (direct from the oven), the cloves and the remaining 200ml of water. Bring back to the boil for a short while. The caramel will be transformed into a thick syrup. Simmer for 10 minutes, then add the pears and continue simmering for a further 20 minutes. Remove from the heat. Cover and leave to marinate in the syrup for at least half a day or longer.

Approx 1 Hour Before Serving
Preheat the oven to 180ºC (fan), 200ºC (non-fan), or gas mark 6.

Drain the pears from their marinade using a slotted spoon and place to one side. Retain the syrup.

Take the 100g of crème pâtissière and mix in the alcohol and pistachios. Put the mixture into a piping bag with a long pointed nozzle (no. 230 if possible, but not essential). Carefully pipe the crème pâtissière into the pears, in the hollows where the cores were. Set to one side.

Roll out 4 sheets of puff pastry to approx 2½ times the size of the pears and place a pear on each. Leaving the stalks exposed, tightly cover the pears with the pastry and place on a baking tray. Glaze the pastry all over with the syrup using a pastry brush. Bake for 10 minutes, or until the pastry is nice and golden in colour. Remove from the oven and allow to cool a little before decorating with some seasonal berries then serve.

Éclair au Chocolat
Chocolate Éclairs

The éclair probably originated during the 19th Century in France, where it was called 'pain à la duchesse' or 'petite duchesse' until 1850, but some chefs think it was first created even earlier than this!

Serves: **4**
Preparation Time: **30 minutes**
Cooking Time: **40 minutes**

Ingredients

For The Éclairs
100ml water
150ml milk
salt (pinch of)
1 tsp sugar
85g butter
2 tsp extra virgin rapeseed oil
150g plain flour
4 eggs

For The Filling
300g crème pâtissière
(see page 268)
3 tsp cocoa powder
1 tsp dark rum

For The Glaze
200g dark chocolate
1 tsp rapeseed oil
1 tsp honey
30g cocoa powder

Chef's Tip

Add chilli powder or used coffee granules to the chocolate filling for a different flavour.

Method

Preheat the oven to 200ºC (fan), 220ºC (non-fan), or gas mark 7.

For The Éclairs
Using a saucepan and only a wooden spoon to mix, bring the water and milk to the boil, then reduce the heat to a simmer. Add the salt, sugar, butter and oil and mix thoroughly. As soon as the butter is completely dissolved, add the flour and heat for a further 2 minutes, stirring (known as banging) the mixture continuously - this prevents the dough from sticking to the sides, but steams the liquid out of the mixture. Set aside to cool.

In a bowl, whisk the eggs together, then add a little to the cooled dough mixture, the equivalent of 1 egg at a time. Mix thoroughly until all the beaten eggs have been used and mixed into the dough.

Place into a piping bag. Using a non-stick baking tray, or a baking tray covered with a silicon sheet, pipe 8 evenly sized cylinders with space around each one as they will expand in the oven. Bake at 200ºC for 10 minutes and then reduce to 180ºC for 10 minutes. Remove and place on a cooling grill.

For The Filling
While the éclairs are baking, warm up the rum (but do not boil), mix in the cocoa powder, add the crème pâtissière and mix thoroughly. Place into a piping bag. Once the éclairs are baked and cooled, use the pointed fitting for the piping bag and pipe the crème pâtissière inside the éclairs. Set aside to glaze.

For The Glaze
Melt the dark chocolate over a bain marie (not boiling, lip temperature - 45ºC). Add the oil, honey and cocoa powder and warm gently. Then using a plastic spatula, spread the sauce over the éclairs and allow to set.

Far Fourn Breton
Baked Raisin Flan

This dish was first introduced to me in the early 80s by the mother of my very dear old friend from Brittany, Jean Louis Farjot.

Serves: **6**
Preparation Time: **15 minutes**
Cooking Time: **70 minutes**

Ingredients

200g raisins
700ml semi-skimmed milk
2 tbsp rum (or whisky)
100g plain flour
100g brown sugar
1 vanilla pod (halved lengthways)
1½ tsp baking powder
4 eggs (beaten)
50g pistachio nuts (shelled)

Method

Preheat the oven to 200°C (fan), 220°C (non-fan), or gas mark 7.

Pour around 100ml of the milk into a saucepan along with the raisins and warm gently. Once simmering, remove from the heat and allow the raisins to inflate, absorbing some of the liquid. Once the raisins are nice and juicy, strain them over a bowl, retaining the liquid. Add the rum to the raisins and set to one side.

Put the strained liquid into the pan with the remaining 600ml of milk and warm gently. Once warm, turn off the heat.

In another mixing bowl, combine the flour, sugar, vanilla pod and baking powder and mix thoroughly.

Add a little of the beaten egg and stir into the flour mix. Add a little more egg and stir again. Repeat this until all the egg has been added.

Using a wooden spoon, pour a little of the milk into the bowl and stir vigorously until combined in full.

Pour the mixture into a baking/gratin dish and bake for 20 minutes. Remove, then add the raisins, sprinkling them over the entire dish. Roughly chop the pistachio nuts and sprinkle them over the top as well. Reduce the oven to 180°C (fan), 200°C (non-fan), or gas mark 6 and bake the flan for a further 20 minutes.

Serve with ice cream.

Chef's Tip

This popular dish can be prepared with any hard fruits like plums or apricots, but it is probably best known with prunes. All variations taste as good as each other.

Flocon d'Avoine
Rolled Oats with Passion Fruit & Coconut Milk

This is a tasty option for a dessert using only natural ingredients.

Serves: **4-6**
Preparation Time: **10 minutes**
Cooking Time: **45 minutes**

Ingredients

300g rolled oats
6 green cardamom pods
300ml full-fat milk
400ml coconut milk
2 tbsp honey
1 star anise
1 vanilla pod (halved lengthways)
80-100g sultanas
3 tbsp crème fraîche
3 passion fruits
¼ lemon (juice of)

Chef's Tip

As an alternative to sultanas, dried raspberries can be used to add colour and flavour. Likewise, crème fraîche can be substituted with fromage blanc to achieve a creamier texture.

Method

Preheat the oven to 160ºC (fan), 180ºC (non-fan), gas mark 4.

This is important! Before you do anything, place the oats and cardamom pods onto a baking tray. Place them in the preheated oven for approx 20 minutes to dry out completely.

Heat the milk gently in a milk pan, adding the coconut milk, honey, star anise, cardamom pods, the vanilla pod and the sultanas. Simmer on a low heat for approx 15 minutes, stirring occasionally. As the milk starts to thicken, add the oats and stir. After a further 15 minutes, remove from the heat and set to one side.

In a bowl, slowly mix the crème fraîche with the flesh of the passion fruits. Add a squeeze of lemon juice to add a 'kick'.

To Serve
Spoon the oats into a bowl and serve with a good dollop of the crème fraîche mixture.

Forêt Noire
Black Forest Cake

Serves: **8**
Preparation Time: **25 minutes**
Cooking Time: **45 minutes**
Fridge: **2 hours**

Ingredients

200g tinned cherries
(strained and the juice retained)
60g honey
1 tbsp Kirsch
1 tbsp fresh mint (chopped)
8 eggs
200g sugar
175g self-raising flour
40g cocoa powder
350g mascarpone cheese
(fresh and kept very cold)
20g flaked almonds
(optional)
20g 70% cocoa dark chocolate
(to decorate)

24cm cake mould

Method

Preheat the oven to 200ºC (fan), 220ºC (non-fan),
or gas mark 7.

Prepare a round, 24cm cake mould by spreading over a
little rapeseed oil with a piece of kitchen paper.

To Start The Filling
In a pan, bring half of the cherry juice from the tin to the
boil and reduce by half until it thickens. Once cool,
add 1 teaspoon of the honey, the cherries, Kirsch and the
mint. Cover with clingfilm and keep in the fridge.

Chef's Tip

Put your glass serving dish into the freezer for at least 2 hours before using - this will help the setting process. Boil the cherries in approx half the juice from their tin and add before spreading over the cake.

Some of the syrup can be poured over the sponge to keep it moist before covering with the mascarpone mixture.

This recipe originates from 1915, created by a man called Josef Keller from Bad Godesberg, Germany.

To Make The Cake

Whisk the eggs and sugar until fluffy and white.

In a separate mixing bowl, combine the flour and cocoa powder. Add the egg mixture, a little at a time, stirring slowly and gently. Pour the cake mix into the mould and place in the oven for 10 minutes. Then, reduce the temperature to 160°C (fan), 180°C (non-fan), gas mark 4 and cook for a further 30 minutes. Remove and turn out onto a wire grill, so that the air passes all around the cake to cool it. Once cold, slice the cake in two across the width. Place one slice onto a cold, large platter (see tip).

To Complete The Filling And To Serve

Mix the mascarpone with the remaining honey. Take your cherry and syrup mixture out of the fridge and combine with the mascarpone. Spread half of this mixture over the base of the cake. Carefully put the other cake slice on top and cover with the remaining mixture.

Decorate with shavings of dark chocolate and, if using, sprinkle over the almonds. Place in the fridge for at least 1 hour.

Galette des Rois
Kings' Cake

Traditionally, this cake is known in the north of France as the 'Galette' and in the south 'Gâteaux des Rois', but is nearly always associated with Christmas and in particular the biblical three kings. When I was younger, I worked as a baker, and one of the first things I was taught was how to make this delicious recipe!

Serves: **6-8**
Preparation Time: **20 minutes**
Rest In Fridge: **30 minutes**
Cooking Time: **40 minutes**

Ingredients

50g unsalted butter (softened)
3 tsp extra virgin rapeseed oil
(or peanut oil)
60g sugar
250g ground almonds
½ vanilla pod (seeds of)
2 eggs
50ml rum
3 tsp honey
2 x 250g sheets puff pastry
1 lemon (juice of, optional - see tip)

Chef's Tip

The juice of 1 lemon can be added to the filling before mixing to give it extra flavour.

Any shaped mould can be used and can be fun for kids to bake.

Method

Preheat the oven to 200ºC (fan), 220ºC (non-fan), or gas mark 7.

Using an electric hand mixer and mixing bowl (stainless steel or glass), mix together the following: butter, oil, sugar, vanilla seeds, honey and ground almonds. Once everything has been blended nicely together add the eggs, one by one, making sure that between eggs everything is mixed together. Finally, add the rum and mix again. Place the mixture into the fridge for at least 30 minutes before using.

When ready to finish the dessert, roll out the puff pastry, on a light dusting of flour, into 2 discs of approx 24cm diameter. On 1 sheet of pastry place some of the filling and spread out evenly to within approx 2cm from the edges. Then, place the other sheet of pastry over the bottom filled sheet and, using 2 sets of fingers, pinch the 2 sheets of pastry together to seal it completely.

Place the pastry onto a silicon sheet or greaseproof paper and place in the oven for 40 minutes. Remove and serve immediately.

Gâteau au Fromage Blanc au Chocolat
Lightweight Chocolate Cheesecake

This recipe uses one of my favourite ingredients, fromage blanc, sometimes called fromage frais, which, if nothing is added, should be virtually fat free.

Serves: **4**
Preparation Time: **30 minutes**
Cooking Time: **50 minutes**

Ingredients

300g pâte brisée (see page 270)
100ml double cream
300g white chocolate
400g fromage blanc
20g cornflour
(mixed with a little cold water)
1 egg (beaten)
150g raspberries
(a few crushed with juice)
20ml Kirsch

24cm deep spring sided cake tin

Method

Preheat the oven to 180°C (fan), 200°C (non-fan), or gas mark 6.

Roll out the pâte brisée so that it is large enough to place inside the mould and a little up the sides of the mould. Blind bake for 15 minutes. Remove from the oven and set aside.

Using a saucepan, gently warm the chocolate and cream (to approx 45°C, otherwise known as lip temperature). Add the fromage blanc with the cornflour and mix thoroughly with a wooden spoon. Remove from the heat. Add the beaten egg and stir again, then add the juice from the raspberries and the Kirsch. Just before pouring the mixture into the mould, gently fold in the raspberries, adding a few at a time.

To Serve
Bake the gâteau for 20-30 minutes (depending on the oven used). The edges should raise by about 3cm or higher. Once it is finished, remove from the oven. Allow to cool before removing from the mould so it sets properly. Serve cold.

Gâteau de Patates Douces et Carottes
Sweet Potato & Carrot Gâteau

Serves: **4-6**
Preparation Time: **20 minutes**
Cooking Time: **2 hours**

Ingredients

120g sweet potatoes (grated)
110g carrots (unpeeled and grated)
250g strong bread flour
(T65 plain flour)
90ml extra virgin olive oil
75g unsalted butter (softened)
225g white sugar
3 eggs (whole and beaten together)
75g walnuts (chopped)
10g baking powder
½ vanilla pod
(seeds extracted to use)
1 unwaxed orange (zest only)

1kg loaf tin

Method

Preheat the oven to 160ºC (fan), 180ºC (non-fan), or gas mark 4.

Mix the grated carrot and sweet potatoes with the zest and the vanilla pod along with the seeds. Spread this onto a baking tray and dry out in the oven initially for 10 minutes at 160ºC (fan) and then reduce to 140ºC (fan) for 15 minutes. At this point the smells will be very intense.

Chef's Tip

If unwaxed oranges are not available, blanch the oranges in boiling water for 1 minute before zesting.

It is possible that a dessert similar to this could have been produced around the time of Christopher Columbus, who brought sweet potatoes back from his travels to the New World.

While the grated ingredients are drying out in the oven, thoroughly combine the eggs, flour, sugar, butter, oil and baking powder in a mixing bowl. Then fold in the dried, warm grated ingredients from the oven. Place everything into a non-stick mould of any shape, but preferably a 1kg loaf tin and leave for 15 minutes to allow the flavours to infuse. In the meantime, increase the oven temperature to 180ºC (fan), 200ºC (non-fan), or gas mark 6.

Place the loaf tin into the oven for 10 minutes at 180ºC (fan) and then reduce to 160ºC (fan) for a further 20 minutes if using a 1kg loaf tin. You can check the cake by inserting either a knife or knitting needle and seeing if it comes out clean. Remove and allow to cool in the tin before turning the gâteau out.

Génoise
Traditional French Bourbon Vanilla Sponge Cake

This cake is popular in France, as well as Italy, and named after the city of Genoa. It is renowned for not relying on chemicals to help it rise, large amounts of air are introduced into the mix by vigorous whisking.

Serves: **4**
Preparation Time: **35 minutes**
Cooking Time: **35 minutes**

Ingredients

180g sugar
8 eggs
80g unsalted butter (melted)
220g plain flour
½ vanilla pod
(split in two, using the seeds)

24cm cake mould

Chef's Tip

A basic Génoise can be sliced into 2 pieces and filled with fresh seasonal fruits and a little whipped cream to create a perfect cake. Cocoa powder can be added during the mix to create a chocolate cake.

Method

Preheat the oven to 180°C (fan), 200°C (non-fan), or gas mark 6.

Create a bain marie on the hob by heating some water in a pan and placing a glass mixing bowl over the pan. Do not boil the water but keep it at approx 45°C (lip temperature).

Put all of the eggs and sugar into the bowl over the bain marie and whisk vigorously for approx 10-15 minutes until it becomes a thick emulsion. Remove from the heat, then slowly mix in the butter and vanilla seeds.

Introduce the flour to the mixture whilst stirring continuously, sprinkling the flour over the bowl a little at a time. It is important to keep stirring and the mixture shouldn't change consistency.

Place the mixture into a 24cm mould lined with greaseproof paper and bake for 30-35 minutes until a knife or skewer comes out clean when inserted.

Remove from the oven and turn out onto a cooling grill.

Kugelhopf
Prune & Raisin Kugelhopf

Marie Antoinette brought this sweet cake from Austria to France when she married Louis XVI. It is still made in Austria, where it is called 'Gugelhupf'.

Serves: **8**
Preparation Time: **20 minutes**
Soak the fruit overnight
Cooking Time: **50 minutes**

Ingredients

15g fresh yeast
90ml full-fat milk
300g plain strong flour
35g granulated sugar
2 large eggs (whole and beaten)
200g unsalted butter (softened)

Prepare The Day Before

50g raisins
30g pitted prunes
(chopped to the same size as raisins)
2 tsp Kirsch

icing sugar (to dust)

Kugelhopf mould

Chef's Tip

Adding flaked almonds on top of the dough before baking will give the cake a different dimension of taste.

Method

Preferably The Night Before Baking
Mix the raisins and prunes together and microwave for 2 minutes. Add the Kirsch and cover with clingfilm. Leave overnight.

On The Baking Day
In a pan, gently warm the milk and yeast together (no boiling).

In a large mixing bowl, combine the sugar, flour and eggs then slowly add the warm milk mixture. If available, use an electric mixer (on a dough hook setting) and mix for approx 10 minutes. Alternatively, hand mixing with a wooden spoon will burn a few more calories, although this may take a little longer! Cover with a cloth and leave to prove in a warm place.

After 1 hour, take the cake dough out of the bowl and knead gently once, then add the fruit mixture (which should be slightly warmed). Place the dough into a non-stick Kugelhopf mould. Once again, cover with a cloth and allow to prove for a further 1 hour.

To Bake
Preheat the oven to 180°C (fan), 200°C (non-fan), or gas mark 6.

Bake the Kugelhopf for initially 15 minutes, then reduce to 160°C (fan) for a further 25 minutes.

Check that a knife or knitting needle comes out clean when inserted into the cake. When finished, turn out onto a cooling grill to cool. Dust with icing sugar and serve.

Madeleines
Small Sponge Cakes

There's a little conflict as to the heritage of this recipe but it's safe to say that it originates from the Lorraine region of north-eastern France.

Serves: **4**
Preparation Time: **25 minutes**
Cooking Time: **10 minutes**

Ingredients

150g unsalted butter
35ml olive oil
2 tsp honey
200g sugar
½ lemon (zest and juice of)
½ tsp fresh thyme leaves
220g plain flour
1 tsp baking powder
3 eggs (beaten)

Chef's Tip

After being in the fridge, and before baking, flaked almonds, crushed pistachios or fresh thyme leaves can be sprinkled over the cakes to give another dimension to these wonderful, miniature cakes.

Method

Heat the butter and oil in a deep pan until it changes to a nutty dark brown colour. Remove from the heat. Then, add the honey, sugar, lemon juice, zest and thyme leaves. Mix with a wooden spatula and slowly add the flour and baking powder. Mix well.

Introduce the beaten eggs and continue to mix vigorously until you have a thick, creamy consistency.

Using a madeleine mould, if possible, fill the moulds and cover with clingfilm. Place into the fridge for as long as possible (overnight is ideal).

Before Baking
Preheat the oven to 200°C (fan), 220°C (non-fan), or gas mark 7.

Remove the clingfilm and place the tray into the oven. Bake for 8-10 minutes (depending on oven being used). When slightly golden in colour, remove and allow to rest. It is very important that they are cool before removing them from the tray.

Maman Novelli
Monique's Pudding

My mother would make this pudding as a festive dessert.

Serves: **6**
Preparation Time: **30 minutes**
Cooking Time: **40 minutes**
Resting Time: **2 hours**

Ingredients

For The Pudding
450ml full-fat milk
175g raisins
125g dried fruits
(a mix of cherries and angelica is perfect)
4 eggs
80g sugar
50ml rum
80g roasted walnuts (crushed)
220g sponge fingers, bread,
or brioche (broken into rough pieces)
2 tsp honey

For The Caramel Base
100g sugar
2 tbsp honey

24cm pudding bowl or 4 jars
(see tip)

Chef's Tip

A little squeeze of half a lemon
and a pinch of chilli powder can
be added to the caramel to give
the cake a totally different taste.
Definitely worth a try!

Try using small jam jars in a
bain marie instead of a large
pudding bowl.

Method

Preheat the oven to 180ºC (fan), 200ºC (non-fan),
or gas mark 6.

For The Pudding
Put 200ml of the milk into a saucepan and bring to
the boil. Add the raisins and dried fruits and simmer for
2 minutes. Using a slotted spoon, remove the fruits from
the warm milk and set aside.

Whisk together the eggs and sugar in a mixing bowl.
Then whisk in the remaining milk (250ml). Add the sponge
fingers, bread or brioche and stir in the nuts and rum.

Add the fruits and some of the warm milk to the bread
mixture.

For The Caramel
In a pan, gently heat the honey and then add the sugar.
Heat this until the colour changes to a golden caramel
colour, then it is complete.

Whilst the caramel is warm and runny, pour it into a
pudding shaped bowl, approx 24cm in diameter, or jars
(see tip). Allow to cool and set.

To Finish
Using a slotted spoon, remove the bread and fruits from the
milk and place on top of the caramel. Finally, pour the milk
mixture over the entire mould, covering the bread and fruits.

Creating A Bain Marie
Place the pudding bowl or jars into a deep baking tray,
which is larger than the mould. Pour water into the larger
tray to approx halfway up the cake mould, to create a bain
marie. Bake for 40 minutes in the oven. After 40 minutes,
the pudding should wobble in the middle when shaken
slightly. Once this happens, remove from the oven and
turn out onto a plate and serve warm. Alternatively, allow
to cool and place in the fridge for at least 2 hours to set
and serve chilled.

Millefeuille au Citron et Fruit de la Passion
Lemon Curd & Passion Fruit Multi-Layered Pastry Slice

The origins of this particular pastry are a little unknown, but the meaning of 'millefeuille' is thousands of leaves.

Serves: **4**
Preparation Time: **30 minutes**
Cooking Time: **30 minutes**

Ingredients

350g ready-made puff pastry
1 tbsp brown sugar
2 lemons (juice of)
110g sugar
3 eggs (beaten)
50g unsalted butter (melted)
4 passion fruits (flesh removed)
1 tsp icing sugar (to dust)

Chef's Tip

If the passion fruits are particularly juicy, add more flesh than juice to the mixture to ensure the sauce remains nice and thick. When piping the dots of lemon curd over the pastry, you can add fresh raspberries or strawberries to change the look and taste of this dessert.

Method

Preheat the oven to 200°C (fan), 220°C (non-fan), or gas mark 7.

For The Pastry
You will need 2 baking trays of the same size, one that can fit snugly on top of the other, plus 2 silicon or baking sheets cut to size. On a lightly floured worktop or board, roll out the pastry to approx 2mm thick. Prick the pastry with a fork to stop it from rising and place onto a lined baking tray. Place the tray into the oven and bake for 5 minutes. Remove the tray and carefully place the other sheet of silicon over the pastry, followed by the other tray. Place as much weight over the tray as possible - even putting it on the floor, placing a cloth over it and standing on the tray if possible. This ensures that the pastry is compacted (very important!). Remove the top tray and silicon then return to the oven for a further 5 minutes. Repeat the process once more before sprinkling with brown sugar. Place back in the oven for a final 5 minutes. Remove from the oven. In total, the pastry should have been in the oven for 15 minutes. Before it cools completely, cut the pastry into 3 equal shaped pieces and allow to cool on a grill.

For The Lemon Curd
Gently warm the lemon juice (do not boil). In a mixing bowl, add the sugar, beaten eggs and melted butter. Mix well, then add this to the warming lemon juice. Bring to a simmer, stirring continuously to thicken. When bubbles start to appear around the edges and the sauce is thickening, add the passion fruit flesh. Remove from the heat, but keep stirring as this will continue to thicken. Place the pan into the fridge to allow to cool completely.

To Assemble
Fill a piping bag with the lemon curd from the fridge. Pipe large dots across the three sheets of pastry, place one on top of the other and serve with a dusting of icing sugar.

Mousse au Chocolat avec Points de Café
Chocolate Mousse with Ground Coffee Granules

A mousse is anything that incorporates bubbles of air and can be sweet or savoury.

Serves: **4**
Preparation Time: **20 minutes**
Fridge Time: **4 hours**

Ingredients

100g dark chocolate
25g organic cocoa powder
(I like to use Green & Blacks)
1 tbsp honey
4 large, very fresh eggs
(yolks and whites separated)
salt (pinch of)
1 tbsp sugar
1 tbsp whisky
2 tsp used coffee granules
½ tsp mild chilli powder

Chef's Tip

45ºC is easy to figure out as it is the temperature which your lips can tolerate heat without scalding yourself. Therefore, you should be able to place it directly onto your lips without burning!

Method

Very important - when making this recipe, only use a wooden or plastic spatula and never metal.

Using a bain marie (bowl over hot water), where the water temperature is approx 45ºC (see tip), melt the chocolate. Add the honey and cocoa powder and whisk thoroughly, then slowly add the whisky.

In a separate bowl, whisk the egg whites with the pinch of salt (to help solidify). When you can see the whisk marks in the egg whites, add the sugar and continue to whisk to stiff peaks.

Beat the yolks in another bowl.

Take approx one third of the beaten yolks, add them to the chocolate sauce and whisk vigorously. Mix in the remaining yolks and the coffee granules and leave to one side.
Add the chilli powder just before mixing with the meringue.

Fold one third of the meringue into the chocolate sauce, then the remainder gets dropped into the mixture folding only once more.

Spoon into dessert bowls and chill for up to 4 hours in the fridge.

245

Panforte à l'Ananas et Chocolat
Pineapple & Chocolate Panforte

This dessert was served to the Queen of Italy, Margherita of Savoy, in 1879.

Serves: **6**
Preparation Time: **40 minutes**
Cooking Time: **30 minutes**

Ingredients

150g dried pineapple (chopped)
70g dried pitted prunes (chopped)
70g raisins (chopped)
220g Brazil nuts
(toasted in a dry pan and chopped)
2 tbsp whisky or Cognac
70g plain flour
2 tbsp dark, bitter
chocolate powder
120g brown sugar
½ red bird's eye chilli
1 tbsp honey
60-80g fromage blanc (to serve)

24cm cake mould

Chef's Tip

Chillies are not always necessary in this recipe, so if you prefer less spice, just leave it out.

Method

Preheat the oven to 160ºC (fan), 180ºC (non-fan), gas mark 4.

Prepare a 24cm cake mould with greaseproof paper on the base.

In a mixing bowl, combine the chopped pineapple, chopped prunes, chopped raisins, toasted chopped nuts and the alcohol. Fold in the flour, chocolate powder and brown sugar.

Slowly heat the honey and oil in a pan. Infuse this with the bird's eye chilli. The chilli can be left to infuse for 2 minutes or more - depending on how spicy you like it - or it can also be left out! Add this to the original mixing bowl with the flour mixture and fold in.

Pour the mixture into the mould and bake for 30 minutes.

Allow to cool down completely. Serve with fromage blanc.

Poire au Vin Rouge
Pears Poached in Red Wine

This dish was invented at the beginning of the 18th Century as another use for Beaujolais wine!

Serves: **4**
Preparation Time: **10 minutes**
Cooking Time: **30 minutes**
Fridge Time: ½ **day**

Ingredients

4 pears (halved, unpeeled)
2 bay leaves
2 black peppercorns
100g brown sugar
400ml Beaujolais wine
1 star anise
1 tsp honey
1 tsp extra virgin rapeseed oil
low fat crème fraîche

Chef's Tip

The rapeseed oil gives the sauce a good glaze and lifts the colours of the fruit.

Method

Put all of the ingredients into a deep pan, with a lid, and bring to the boil. Reduce the heat to a simmer for 30 minutes with the lid on. Remove from the heat and, when cool, place into the fridge for up to half a day WITHOUT removing the lid.

To Serve
Remove the pan from the fridge, remove the pears and heat the sauce gently. Reduce the sauce to thicken. Taste the sauce and, if required, add a little honey. Add the rapeseed oil and pour over the pears, which have now been placed on a plate, ready for serving.
Serve with a spoonful of low fat crème fraîche.

Riz au Jus d'Orange au Four
Baked Rice Pudding in Orange Juice

Popular during Halloween as the dish goes quite orange due to the amount of juice used.

Serves: **6-8**
Preparation Time: **10 minutes**
Cooking Time: **80 minutes**

Ingredients

250g dessert or Arborio rice
1ltr freshly squeezed orange juice
1 vanilla pod (halved lengthways)
1 bay leaf
1 sprig rosemary
200g raisins
100ml fromage blanc

Chef's Tip

This dish has had all the major fat (ie milk) substituted with the orange juice and it still has a great effect. Wonderful on a cold winter's night.

Introduce sliced, unwaxed oranges, cut into quarters, during the final 5 minutes of cooking. This will help to glaze the dish and make it look fantastic when served.

Method

Preheat the oven to 160°C (fan), 180°C (non-fan), or gas mark 4.

Bring the orange juice to the boil in a pan and add the vanilla pod, bay leaf and rosemary. Simmer for 15 minutes. Finally, add the raisins and the rice and infuse for 5 minutes.

Place the rice and orange mixture into a gratin dish and bake for 1 hour. Serve with a little fromage blanc.

Tarte au Sucre
Sugar Tart

This tart is popular in many French speaking areas, not only in Europe, but Canada too!

Serves: **4**
Preparation Time: **20 minutes**
Plus 2 hours proving time
Cooking Time: **45-60 minutes**

Ingredients

400g strong plain flour
5 egg yolks (lightly beaten)
130g unsalted butter (softened)
80ml full-fat milk
15g baker's yeast
(baking powder can be substituted)
1½ tbsp granulated sugar
1 cinnamon stick

For The Glaze
Part 1 - 150g brown sugar
(cassonade if possible)

Part 2 - 2 eggs (beaten together) mixed with 80ml crème fraîche

Method

For The Tart
In a pan, gently warm the milk, yeast and 1½ tablespoons of sugar with the cinnamon stick, then stir.

In another large bowl, mix the flour, softened butter and egg yolks, then slowly add the warm cinnamon infused milk mixture until a dough consistency is achieved.
Set the bowl aside in a warm place with a cloth covering it and allow to prove for 1 hour. The dough should double in size.

Take the dough out of the bowl and bang it on the worktop. Knead once to remove the build-up of gases. Place the dough into a non-stick fluted mould (Tourtière).

For The Glaze
Sprinkle with 150g brown sugar (cassonade) then cover with a cloth. Allow to prove for another 30-60 minutes.

In the meantime, preheat the oven to 200ºC (fan), 220ºC (non-fan), or gas mark 7.

Just before the dough is ready to go into the oven, pour the beaten egg and crème fraîche mixture over the dough, without touching the dough itself. Immediately transfer this to the hot oven. Bake for 15 minutes then reduce to 150ºC (fan) for a further 30 minutes.

Turn out of the mould onto a cooling grill and serve with a little ice cream or crème fraîche.

Tiramisu au Chocolat et Café
Tiramisu with Chocolate & Coffee Granules

This was originally classed as an Italian trifle but is now available all across Europe.

Serves: **6**
Preparation Time: **15 minutes**
Fridge Resting Time: **2 hours**

Ingredients

approx 12 sponge fingers or boudoir biscuits (more maybe required depending on the size of the bowl used. See page 260 for recipe)

2 tbsp espresso coffee (liquid coffee)

1 tbsp used coffee granules (still moist)

5 tbsp Amaretto or whisky

300g mascarpone cheese

125ml confiture de lait (see page 262 for recipe)

½ bar good quality, dark bitter chocolate (shaved with a vegetable peeler - to decorate)

Chef's Tip

Add 40g dried cranberries to the mixture when folding in the confiture de lait for an additional flavour dimension.

Method

Put your glass serving dish in the freezer for at least 2 hours before using.

Place the sponge fingers into a bowl. Mix the espresso coffee with the coffee granules and alcohol, then pour over the biscuits so they absorb the liquid.

In a mixing bowl, whisk the mascarpone, then fold in the confiture de lait.

Remove your glass serving bowl from the freezer and spoon a little mascarpone mixture onto the base. On top of this layer, add all of the soaked biscuits, then another layer of mascarpone to finish. If using individual serving bowls, you can always add more layers.

Place into the fridge for up to 2 hours. Decorate with dark chocolate shavings and serve.

Ze Novelli Academy Tarte Tatin
Baked Apple with Caramel

Created by the Tatin sisters in Sologne in the 19th Century. In a daze, Stephanie Tatin forgot to put pastry into the pan! Noticing her forgetfulness, she decided to add the pastry over the apples and bake the pie and this is the result. Hunters have since enjoyed this pie, which became known as 'Tarte Tatin'.
The original restaurant is still open! And if you visit my Novelli Academy, you will definitely experience my version at some time.

Serves: **4**
Preparation Time: **20 minutes**
Cooking Time: **40 minutes**

Ingredients

5 apples
(peeled and halved, just before using)
100g butter
200g sugar
1 star anise
½ vanilla pod (halved lengthways)
6 cardamom pods
1 large pack ready-made puff pastry

Chef's Tip

After covering and sealing the apples with the pastry and the pastry starts moving around in the pan, it is time to put it into the oven.

Method

Preheat the oven to 180°C (fan), 200°C (non-fan), or gas mark 6.

Using a large ovenproof frying pan (approx 28cm), gently melt the butter on a medium heat with the star anise, vanilla pod and cardamom pods. Add the sugar and gently colour everything until pale yellow in colour.

Peel and slice the apples in half and pat dry with kitchen paper. Place neatly, face down, into the pan and set aside.

Roll out the ready-made puff pastry into a circle, approx 28cm in diameter and ½cm thick. Carefully place the pastry over the entire pan, pressing the pastry all around the apples to form a tight seal. The apples at the edge of the pan can be lifted slightly and the pastry tucked underneath. This will avoid steaming the pastry as opposed to baking it.

Put the pan on a low heat. After a couple of minutes, lift the pan, place your hand over the pastry and, holding it tight, pour off the excess liquid - this is saturated fat that has formed and isn't required. Repeat this process twice before placing the pan into the oven for approx 25-30 minutes. After this time, remove from the oven and leave to rest for about 5 minutes, which will allow the caramel to settle and become firm.

To Serve
Position a lightly oiled plate, which is larger than the pan, over the pan and turn out the tatin, being careful not to spill the caramel that may still be hot. Serve with good quality, real vanilla ice cream.

Biscuit à la Cuillère
Sponge Fingers

These biscuits are dry and sweet, elongated and sprinkled with icing sugar. They are used primarily in the making of charlottes and tiramisu.

Serves: **6**
Preparation Time: **40 minutes**
Cooking Time: **10 minutes**

Ingredients

6 eggs (yolks and whites separated, kept very cold)
140g sugar
1 tbsp Kirsch
salt (pinch of)
140g plain flour
icing sugar (to dust)

Method

Preheat the oven to 160ºC (fan), 180ºC (non-fan), or gas mark 4.

In a large glass or stainless steel mixing bowl, whisk the egg yolks and add 40g of the sugar. Mix thoroughly, then add a drop of the Kirsch and mix again.

In a separate glass or stainless steel bowl, whisk the egg whites. When you start seeing the whisk marks in the mixture, add the remaining 100g of sugar and a pinch of salt. Whisk quickly until very firm. Slowly whisk in the flour.

Put 1 large spoonful of the whisked egg white (meringue mixture) into the egg yolk mixture and mix thoroughly (with a wooden/plastic spatula, not metal). Fold the remaining meringue into the yolks mixture. Put all of the mixture into a piping bag and place into the freezer for at least 30 minutes, if using immediately. If using the next day, leave it in the fridge overnight.

Using either a non-stick baking tray, or silicon sheet on a baking tray, pipe 5cm long cylinders onto the tray - leave a gap in-between each one and bake for 12-15 minutes, or until firm to the touch.

Remove from the oven and, when cool, sprinkle with icing sugar. These can be used in a number of recipes, or alone with ice cream.

Chef's Tip

When whisking the egg whites, as soon as you add the pinch of salt, you must whisk immediately without stopping. When whisking, do not touch the base of the bowl and lift the whisk in and out of the top of whatever you are whisking for a quicker result.

Confiture de Lait
Slowly Cooked, Sweetened Milk

This accompaniment was originally created by French explorers returning from South America. French chefs found many uses for this versatile dessert ingredient.

Serves: **As required**
Preparation Time: **15 minutes**
Cooking Time: **60-90 minutes**

Ingredients

1ltr full-fat milk
1 tbsp cornflour
400g white granulated sugar
20ml water
½ vanilla pod or
1 cinnamon stick

Chef's Tip

If speed is of the essence then simply replace the milk with 410ml tinned evaporated milk and 400ml full-fat milk, which will compensate for the reduction time.

Method

Gently heat the sugar and water together, in a pan. Simmer until the mixture turns into a golden colour.

In the meantime, in another non-stick pan, heat the milk with the vanilla or cinnamon. Using a little of the warm milk in a glass, mix the cornflour into a paste and then reintroduce this into the milk and stir. Bring back to simmering point then slowly introduce the golden sugar mix, a little at a time, to the warm milk. This may splatter a little so be careful.

Simmer and cook for 1 hour, stirring every 15 minutes until the last 10 minutes of cooking. At this point you will need to stir more frequently to avoid the confiture de lait sticking to the bottom of the pan.

After 1 hour it should reach the consistency of custard. Pour into a Kilner-type jar. It will keep in the fridge for up to 7 days.

263

Crème Anglaise
Sweet Custard

Apparently this method of using eggs to thicken cream dates back to the Roman times and is named after the English because of their love of sweet things.

Serves: **4**
Preparation Time: **10 minutes**
Cooking Time: **15 minutes**

Ingredients

1 whole egg
2 egg yolks
75g sugar
500ml full-fat milk
½ vanilla pod
(halved lengthways, seeds scraped out)

Chef's Tip

If your sauce happens to curdle, place all the sauce (milk mixture) into a jar, close the lid tightly and shake. The crème should go back to normal after a little while of shaking. Be careful when opening the jar!

Method

Beat the whole egg and egg yolks together, then add the sugar. Mix until it reaches a yellow ribbon texture.

Bring the milk to the boil in a milk pan. Simmer for 2 minutes, then remove from the heat.

Pour a little hot milk into the egg mixture and whisk vigorously, then add the rest of the milk and whisk. Pour the combined mixture back into the pan and heat gently until the sauce thickens, stirring occasionally with a wooden spoon. Once the sauce is thick enough to coat the back of the spoon, add the vanilla seeds and stir again. Remove from the heat. Your sweet custard is ready to use.

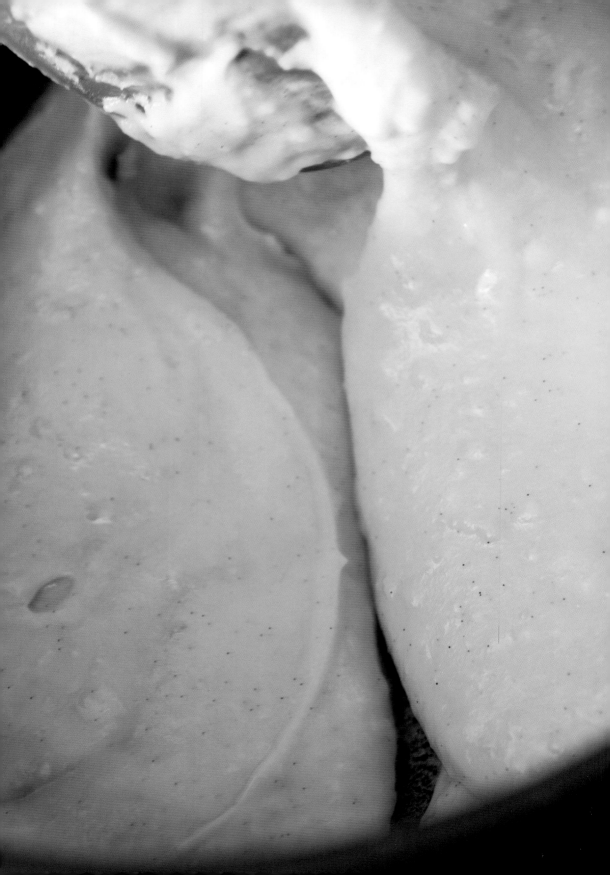

Crème Pâtissière
Vanilla Pastry Cream

This rich, thick custard has been developed over many years of patisserie making and everyone has their own methods of perfecting this versatile cream. This is my simple way!

Serves: **4**
Preparation Time: **20 minutes**
Cooking Time: **15 minutes**

Ingredients

1ltr full-fat milk
1 vanilla pod (halved lengthways)
2 egg yolks
3 eggs
1 tsp extra virgin rapeseed oil
180g unrefined caster sugar
125g plain flour
1 lemon (juice of)

Chef's Tip

Crème pâtissière can be used in many ways, including as a base for tarts using strawberries or other summer fruits.

Method

Using a milk pan, heat the milk and split vanilla pod, but do not let it boil. As soon as a simmer is reached, remove from the heat and allow the vanilla to infuse in the milk.

Whisk all the eggs and egg yolks in a bowl. Add the sugar and oil, whisk until creamy. Slowly add the flour and mix thoroughly (a wooden spatula may be required at this stage). Slowly add about half the warm milk and whisk/stir again. When completely mixed into the sauce, add the remaining milk. Stir in completely. Return the vanilla cream back into the original pan and heat to a simmer.

Stir continuously, but only with a wooden spoon, and watch the sauce thicken. Tiny bubbles should form around the pan where it meets the sauce. When the bubbles appear, taste the sauce and, if required, add a squeeze of lemon juice to balance the sweetness. Allow the sauce to cool down. Set aside in the fridge before using.

Pâte Brisée
Pastry Base

This versatile base is used in various French recipes such as Quiche Lorraine or Tarte Normande.

Serves: **As required**
Preparation Time: **20 minutes**
Cooking Time: **25 minutes**
Resting Time: **60 minutes**

Ingredients

200g plain flour
2 tsp extra virgin rapeseed oil
1 egg
20-25ml water (chilled)
80g unsalted butter (softened)
½ tsp salt
½ tsp honey

24cm flan mould

Chef's Tip

This is the perfect base for many types of tart, sweet or savoury.

Method

Preheat the oven to 200°C (fan), 220°C, (non-fan), or gas mark 7.

In a large glass or stainless steel bowl, mix the flour, salt, honey, butter, oil and egg. Gradually add the chilled water - mix in enough water until a dough starts to form.
Then, using a lightly floured work top, roll the dough flat. Either roll out a little larger than your mould, then place into the mould, or roll out over a plate and cover with clingfilm. Place in a fridge until required.

Remove the dough from the fridge at least 30 minutes before using to reach room temperature. Blind baking beans, or anything else that is available these days for blind baking, are not necessary. Instead, take a clean kitchen cloth and press the dough down from the centre of the baking mould towards the edges. This removes the humidity that may be in the pastry.

Place into the hot oven for 15 minutes. If the pastry has not changed colour, reduce the oven temperature to 160°C (fan), 180°C (non-fan), or gas mark 4 and bake for a further 10 minutes. When cooked, pat with a dry cloth.

Langues de Chat
The Cat's Tongue Biscuits

Translated, this actually means the cat's tongue and has been made in and around Europe since 1900.

Serves: **4**
Preparation Time: **20 minutes**
Cooking Time: **10 minutes**

Ingredients

130g unsalted butter (softened)
75g sugar
3 eggs (beaten)
130g plain flour
1 lemon (squeeze of)
50g icing sugar (to dust)

Chef's Tip

Before baking, you can sprinkle some crushed almonds or pistachio nuts over each flattened dough. Also, before allowing the langues de chats to cool completely, they can be moulded around cold stainless steel ladles to create baskets for fruit and ice cream - or even rolling pins to form cylinders. Try it and see!

Method

Mix the softened butter and the sugar with a wooden spoon until you have a smooth paste consistency. Add the beaten eggs and start whisking thoroughly, then add the flour. At the last minute, add a little squeeze of lemon juice - obviously without pips. Mix again with the wooden spoon. When thoroughly mixed, place into the fridge until you are ready to bake.

To Bake
Preheat the oven to 180ºC (fan), 200ºC (non-fan), or gas mark 6.

Line a baking tray with either a sheet of greaseproof paper or a silicon sheet. Spoon a heaped tablespoon of the mixture onto the tray. pipe lines and feather, using a metal spoon, into long tongues. Alternatively, wet a large serving spoon in cold water and flatten the mixture in a circular motion. Repeat with the rest of the dough, flattening each one in the same way.

Bake in the oven for approx 8-10 minutes, checking that they do not burn. Once ready, remove from the oven and place on a wire grill to cool. Dust with icing sugar. They are then ready to use.

Le Crunch
Caramel Crunch

Serves: **As required**
Cooking Time: **5-10 minutes**
Resting Time: **2 hours**

Ingredients

250g sugar (any type)
20ml water

Chef's Tip

Sprinkle the caramel powder
onto the top of any pudding
based dessert and blow torch
until golden.

Method

Heat the sugar and water in a pan until it boils. Once it thickens, pour onto a silicon sheet or lined baking tray (about 2-3mm in thickness) and set aside for at least 2 hours until completely cooled.

Now smash it in any way you wish! Grind in a coffee grinder to form a caramel crunch powder. Store in a jar with a tight fitting lid and it will keep for weeks.

My After 8 O'Clock Treat

This is a little treat that I created for myself to nibble on after a busy day in the Academy, influenced by my friend Dayan's ginger cookies which were more than enjoyed by my fiancée, Michelle, whilst pregnant with our son Jacques.

Serves: **4**
Preparation Time: **20 minutes - the night before using**
Cooking Time: **15 minutes**

Ingredients

120ml full-fat milk
1 tsp ginger root (freshly grated)
2 star anise
1 stick cinnamon
400g plain flour
125g sugar
5g bicarbonate of soda
150g unsalted butter (softened)
50g honey
100g grated coconut
salt (pinch of)

Method

The Night Before

In a saucepan, bring the milk, ginger, star anise and cinnamon to the boil and simmer for 2 minutes. Remove from the heat. Add the flour, sugar, bicarbonate of soda, honey, butter, pinch of salt and coconut and mix thoroughly to create a dough. Leave in the fridge overnight.

Preheat the oven to 180ºC (fan), 200ºC (non-fan), or gas mark 6.

To Bake

Roll the dough, on a lightly floured surface, to 1cm thick and cut rounds from the dough, either by hand or by using a shaped cutter. Place on a baking tray lined with either a silicon sheet or baking paper. Bake in the oven for 10 minutes, then reduce to 160ºC (fan), 180ºC (non-fan), or gas mark 4. Bake for a further 5 minutes, then remove carefully and place onto a wire grill to cool.

Ready to eat after 8 o'clock in the evening as a treat.

Chef's Tip

Instead of ginger, you can experiment with different flavours, eg thyme or cumin seeds, or combinations of spices and herbs - give it a try!

Cutting them into square biscuits works well too but I tend to eat too many that way!

Having had such wonderful support both in the making of this book and loyal suppliers to my Novelli Academy, I must add the following personal thank yous.

Simon Mead, Chiltern Cold Pressed Oil - P E Mead and Sons

www.pemeadandsons.co.uk

Simon has been supplying us with some of the best quality cold pressed extra virgin rapeseed oil for some time now and has been an immense help sourcing and supplying various meats and vegetables both from his own farm and also from his neighbouring suppliers around the Chilterns - including the wood for my oven.

Gerard and Dianne Richardson, Richardsons of Whitehaven

www.richardsonsofwhitehaven.co.uk

Gerard and Dianne have been close friends for many years and have also worked with me on a couple of previous successful and interesting books and there is basically very little they don't know about wine and good food.

Camilla Deane, Bel UK

www.bel-group.com

Bel UK have been great friends of the Academy for several years and have supplied us with such a wide range of fabulous cheeses. Thank you.

Ian Kennedy, IK Fish
www.ikfish.co.uk

Having met Ian and his beautiful family during one of my demos in Durham last year, we instantly bonded and he supplies us with only the best quality fish.

Richard Paul, Bradbury's
www.bradburyscheese.co.uk

Richard has provided us with the best worldwide award-winning cheeses that can be found anywhere and has given us immense support since meeting him at the International Cheese Awards in Nantwich.

Mel Ryan, Gastrolux UK
www.gastrolux.co.uk

Mel has supplied the Academy chefs with a huge range of some of the best quality and most heat resistant pans that are available in the shops today.

Tom Gozney, Gozney Stone Baked Ovens
www.thestonebakeovencompany.co.uk

We chose Gozney Stone Baked Ovens for the Academy a while ago which has proven to be a very popular attraction in many of the courses. The fantastic smells and results speak for themselves.

Ziganof Knives
www.ziganof-knives.com

Ziganof helped me to design my own custom made range of high quality knives available through the Novelli Academy and other outlets.

Marc Raven, Citroën UK
www.citroen.co.uk

Marc and Citroën have supported me for a long time now and have made my travelling around Europe to various functions a pleasure rather than a chore.

Helen, Gillian and Panna from Electrolux/AEG
www.electrolux.co.uk

The fantastic team based in Luton has supported us for many events and have always supplied the highest quality equipment whenever we have needed it.

Paul Mullee, Chiltern Marble
www.chilternmarble.co.uk

Chiltern Marble have supplied the Academy for several years with all of our granite and marble work tops and only supply the best available products, with the granite table being an integral feature in my Academy.

Other contributors that I would like to thank are:

Jo Bottrill
Bread aficionado.

Jonathan Lear, Potash Farm Foods
www.potashfarmfoods.co.uk

George, Wild Game Direct
www.wildgamedirect.co.uk

Robin, Wicks Manor Pork
www.wicksmanor.com

Steve & Jane Gollins
www.freerange-eggs.co.uk

Jo Evans, VHB Herbs
www.vhbherbs.co.uk

Jeremy Palmer, Essential Cuisine
www.essentialcuisine.com

Relish PUBLICATIONS

Relish Publications
www.relishpublications.co.uk

Duncan, Teresa and Vicki their designer, have truly been amazing to work with. To have produced my book within two months from start to finish, only shows how professional a team of people can be. Thank you again.

Tim Green
www.timgreenphotographer.co.uk

Tim is an exceptional personality and a pleasure to work with and the beautiful photographs speak for themselves.

Food & Wine Pairing

Jean-Christophe and I have been friends for a number of years. We share the same passions about food and wine and about breaking down the mysterious barriers to help people try new and exciting flavours.

Pairing wine to food has often been described as an art but let me debunk that theory right now. Taking raw natural ingredients and creating the dishes Jean creates is an art. What I do is a mix of common sense and personal taste. First of all there are general rules, such as white wine with white meat and fish and red wine with red meats and sauces, but that's far too rigid these days. The new world wines that broke into the market in the 80s changed all that forever with soft, juicy, un-tannic Merlots and Shiraz that can be paired with most things if red is what floats your boat.

So, how do you select the perfect match? The main thing is to remember that the food comes first so never overpower it. What you are aiming to do is complement it, rather like a first date. You will get better at it each time you try, and it really is fun to try. Jean concentrates on the fresh, natural flavours of the main ingredients and, with seemingly few additions, he maximises the flavours like no other chef, which makes pairing his creations with wine so delightful.

I'm going to suggest a number of particular wines and hence styles to accompany the recipes in the book.

For Fish
Whitehaven Sauvignon Blanc, Marlborough, New Zealand
The Marlborough Sauvignons are my favourites. Although distant copies of the famous Loire Valley Sancerres, they are softer. More tropical fruit dominates noses with masses of lychees and super ripe crisp fruits on the palate. This is particularly good with the oilier fish such as sardines and mackerel.

The White Viogner, South Australia
Viogner is my secret passion, never having had a poor one, but this version is not only stunningly presented but it's also packed with lavender aromas, with apricots and lemons on the palate. While all these wines will pair across the board, Viogner is particularly attractive with cod-based dishes and soufflé.

Saint Veran, Josephe Drouhin, Burgundy
Possibly my favourite Chardonnay, classy but not a budget buster. Its full, rich fruits and crisp steely finish make it stunning with shellfish, although I need no excuse to partner it with any fish and many duck recipes.

For Meat and Vegetarian
Château Dauzac 5ème Cru Classe, Margaux, Bordeaux
One of the affordable legends of Bordeaux. Complex flavours of black cherry fruit with violets and toasty spice and a superb velvet like texture. My perfect partner for anything with beef or venison in the recipe but it is also particularly impressive with sweet potatoes and smoked aubergines.

Monte Real Tinto Gran Reserva Rioja
There is never a bad time to enjoy this wine. It is smooth with vanilla and caramel, mixed with ripe berries and a long finish. It is quite succulent with many styles of dish but goes particularly well with rich sauces or peppered dishes as well as those heavy with mushrooms.

Gerard Richardson

For Dessert

To be honest, by the time you get to a dessert wine it's a bit like a Downton Abbey dinner but, if you can run the course, the rewards are fabulous. In fact there are many times I would skip the first two courses if I could. Jean's desserts are always rich and full which means you can go straight past many of the wishier-washier pudding wines and straight into the big boys. My favourites at the moment are quite surprising.

Klein Constantia Vin de Constance, South Africa

Okay, it's expensive but this is like coating your tongue in velvet and hosting Strictly Come Dancing in your mouth. So fruity, rich and exciting, the flavours burst out in abundance with each sip. It's literally bursting with marmalade, apricot, nectarine and crème brûlée flavours. Other big fans were Napoleon Bonaparte, Louis XVI of France and a whole boatload of Russian Tsars.

Turkey Flat Pedro Ximenez, Australia

Technically a style of Sherry, PX is the ultimate expression of rich, raisin-style fortified wines and the hotter the climate, the richer and more toffee-like the result. The Turkey Flat PX is so delicious you can even just pour it on ice cream, but if you partner it with Jean's madeleines or crème brûlée the result is a love affair for life.

Gerard and Dianne Richardson, Richardsons of Whitehaven,

Richardsons of Whitehaven are traditional Fine Wine Merchants operating from a beautiful Georgian shop in the historic town of Whitehaven on the West Coast of Cumbria. With a great range of classics, especially Riojas and ports, it's a haven for wine lovers.
www.richardsonsofwhitehaven.co.uk Tel: 01946 65334

What a challenge it is to find the French cheeses demanded by a top French chef!

Having worked with Jean-Christophe through the Novelli Academy for many years, I know that his cheese expectations are high, so I've put together a few little tips and recommendations to guide you through the hazards of choosing cheese.

In the world of cheese there are so many flavours and styles that fit foods and moments throughout any day. I always think with my heart, and go straight to a cheese that would light up any dining occasion.

Epoisses is simply a cheese luxury, being rich, creamy and fruity. The challenge is to get past the characteristic odour. You are missing out on a great product unless you taste it. For me, Berthaut is the best example.

French Comté is a sensational cheese for cooking. It has exploded in the UK in the last few years and is available everywhere, with two distinctive styles. Classic French, which is full-flavoured and savoury, then there is the sweeter profile, with hints of toffee and caramel. If you taste it you will know what I mean. The savoury product is similar to its versatile Swiss cousin, Gruyère, which is most famously used in culinary dishes as it has great flavour impact and fantastic melting qualities.

For fresh and soft cheese usage, goat's cheese has long been the dominant influence in French cookery. Un-rinded fresh goat's cheese needs to be light, fresh and citrusy.

Whisper it quietly so that JCN doesn't hear, but in Britain and Ireland we now have a number of good washed rind cheese such as Golden Cenarth, and Italy too has the unique taste of Tallegio, which is similar in style to French Camembert.

There is a huge selection of British matured Cheddars for you to choose from, but with the rise of sweeter flavours, 'crunchers' and cave-aged, there are now some truly different options. So don't be constrained by favourite brands, try some of the less familiar names and types. For JCN I suggested an 18-month unpasteurised Westcombe Cheddar. Matured to perfection, fruitful and with a brittle texture, which means a small amount gives bags of flavour.

I selected a 24-month Parmesan, not too dry, with good flavours and a hint of sweetness, avoiding that slightly acid finish. A good Grana Padano or a vegetarian hard cheese alternative are easily available.

Mascarpone needs to be rich and creamy with a thick texture.

When selecting a real Greek Feta I'd recommend looking for 100% sheep's milk, the original type, which is softer and creamier of texture, lively and fresh. But why not try crumbing an authentic Cheshire instead of some of these poor over-salted salad cheeses, making your salad lighter and tastier.

Richard Paul, Bradbury's, www.bradburyscheese.co.uk

Conversion Chart

Cooking Temperatures

Degrees Celsius	Fahrenheit	Gas Mark
140	275	1
150	300	2
160-170	325	3
180	350	4
190	375	5
200-210	400	6
220	425	7
230	450	8
240	475	9

*Temperatures for fan-assisted ovens are, as a general rule, normally about 20°C lower than regular oven temperature.

Weight Measurement Conversions

1 teaspoon (5ml/5g)	¼ oz
1 tablespoon (15ml/15g)	¾ oz
10g	½ oz
25g	1oz
50g	2oz
75g	3oz
150g	5oz
200g	7oz
250g	9oz
350g	12oz
450g	1lb
1kg	2.2lb

Volume Measurement Conversions

55ml	2 fl oz
150ml	¼ pt
275ml	½ pint
570ml	1 pt
1 ltr	1¾ pt

"During the production of this book, Jean-Christophe Novelli and his team personally prepared, cooked and tasted every recipe featured. All photographs are of the actual dishes, taken during and after the cooking process."